BECOMING A LIFE ADVISOR

A Guide to the Ultimate Client Service Model

BECOMING A
LIFE ADVISOR

A Guide to the
Ultimate Client Service Model

Rod Hagenbuch
&
Richard J. Capalbo

ISBN 0-9725769-1-6
Printed by Sinclair Printing Company, Los Angeles

First Edition

We dedicate this book to our wives,
LaVerne Hagenbuch and Kathleen Capalbo,
for their decades of support and understanding.

Rod Hagenbuch
and
Richard J. Capalbo

CONTENTS

ABOUT THE AUTHORS

Rod Hagenbuch is co-founder of the Quantum Leap Institute and Quantum Leap Securities. He is a graduate of Michigan State University, attended the Stanford University Executive Management program and is a Certified Financial Manager. He has lectured throughout the country in both the wirehouse and independent sectors on financial advisor management practice and how to use securities research. He has also lectured at the Securities Industry Institute (SII) at the Wharton School of Business at the University of Pennsylvania and at the Milgard School of Business at the University of Washington. He is the co-author, with Richard Capalbo, of "Investment Survival, How to Use Securities Research." Rod's professional experience includes 32 years in the securities industry with Merrill Lynch as an institutional consultant working with Fortune 100 companies, state and municipal retirement funds and over 20 bank trust departments. He managed branch offices in Columbus, Ohio; Tacoma, Washington; and the flagship Los Angeles office. While at Merrill Lynch, Rod served on the board of directors of their California Trust Company. He has hired, trained and managed securities brokers for over 20 years. During the past six years, he has written over a dozen training programs for financial advisors. He has served on over 30 non-profit boards and currently chairs the Greater Los Angeles Red Cross. Rod lives with his wife, LaVerne, in Pacific Palisades, California.

Richard J. Capalbo is a principal in the Quantum Leap Institute LLC, a Los Angeles consulting firm specializing in both the financial service industry and in bringing all access to all aspects of the financial service industry to corporations. He lectures extensively throughout the securities and mutual fund industries. He is the founder of the Quantum Leap Institute and specializes in enhancing individual's behavior by analyzing changing trends and helping individuals adjust to these changes. He is the co-author of a recent book entitled "Investment Survival" which deals with creating portfolios to track various benchmark performances. Mr. Capalbo served as district sales and marketing manager for Merrill Lynch and as co-manager of their flagship Southern California office. Formerly, he was chairman, president and chief executive officer of Bateman, Eichler, Hill, Richards, and Incorporated where he directed its expansion into seven western states, making it the largest regional brokerage

About the Authors

firm headquartered on the West Coast. He also served on the Kemper Financial board of directors. He was previously senior vice president of Drexel Burnham Lambert, with responsibility for the firm's marketing department, which he founded. He began his career in the securities industry using econometrics in Modern Portfolio Theory and lectured extensively on that topic during its developmental years. He has consulted with many of the prominent asset management firms, security firms, banks and insurance companies. From 1979 to 1987, he was an active member of the SIA's Sales and Marketing Committee and in 1986-87 served as its co-chairman. Mr. Capalbo has served as a trustee of the Securities Industry Institute for over a decade; he was chairman of the Institute in 1998-99. He is a guest lecturer at The University of Southern California, The Wharton School and Loyola Marymount University of Los Angeles. He holds a bachelor's degree in economics from Fordham University in New York and a master's degree in finance from the Wharton School of Finance and Commerce of the University of Pennsylvania.

He lives with his wife, Kathleen, in Pasadena, California.

ACKNOWLEDGMENTS

We have drawn on experiences and interaction with many people for both information and inspiration to write this book. The contacts and experiences are both recent and some come from people we interacted with many years ago. Blending the wisdom, insights and information from many people over the past 40 years has allowed us to gain a comprehensive understanding of our industry and to have some serious thoughts about where we are going in the years ahead. We have learned as much as we have taught from the hundreds of financial advisors we have managed. The feedback, suggestions and shared experiences of the thousands of financial advisor we have worked with since forming the Quantum Group in 1999 have provided the breath of knowledge of the industry which has added to our own understanding of the dynamics of servicing clients in all channels of the financial services industry.

The following have been influential in specific topics discussed in this book. We appreciate their insight and with many, long-term friendships.

Larry Biederman, Jon Burnham, Jake Butts, Robert Cialdini, Ph.D., Don Connelly, Robert DeChellis, Charles Dwyer, Ph.D., Gordon Gainer, Dan Garver, Eric Gerth, Jon Goodman Ph.D., Robert Goodman Ph.D., Mark Harper, Douglas Vickers Ph.D., Dean Hutton, Dewitt Jones, Mel Kaufman, Nick Murray, Dan Love, J. Mitchell Perry Ph.D., Sylvan Schefler, Kathy Tricca, Joe Smith, David Solie, Thomas Stanley Ph.D., Jack Surber, and our many friends at Goldman Sachs and the Securities Industry Institute.

Because the book draws on our experiences and events over the past 35 years, we apologize to many people that have contributed to our knowledge who we have may have missed.

Of course, any mistakes are ours alone.

Special thanks go to James Klein, our incredible editor, who significantly improved the content and understandability of what we were trying to say. He was also diplomatic in removing over 100 pages of information which was very interesting to us, but would not have served the interest of our readers.

Thanks also to Sheryl MacPhee, who once again designed and created the cover for the book that pleased us, and converted and copy edited our word documents into the pagination and layout for the book.

INTRODUCTION

We decided to write this book because we never seem to have the time to answer all the questions we get from people about how to position themselves to become true *Life Advisors*. We also came to the conclusion that addressing the issue of helping people with non-financial problems is the biggest challenge and opportunity that advisors have in building their practice. The research we have done to prepare the manuscript for the book, and the many rewrites necessary to complete it, have challenged our own initial thinking and conclusions.

Proving and refining the concept for the book and finally writing it have taken more than a year and a half. During this time, we have had the opportunity to have a number of advisors try out some of our concepts. When making presentations to advisors and conducting workshops, we have received many questions and a lot of feedback from people that are currently active in the business. From the feedback we have gained many suggestions and insights that have contributed significantly to the book and we are grateful for all of their help and practical insights. We knew from our own personal experiences that being a Life Advisor was very important to our own sense of self-worth and success. Having worked with a lot of financial advisors from many different firms now convinces us that those that choose to become Life Advisors will find not only greater success but also a great deal more self-satisfaction in their profession.

We know that financial advisors are questioning our advice just as they are raising questions about the objectivity of securities research. We have received many constructive challenges to our ideas and know that what we are advocating is not totally new. The help we have received from advisors we have worked with this past year has been key in sharpening our focus and seeing if the concepts work in practice with some of the top professionals in the industry. We are pleased that our clients tell us these ideas are sound and greatly enhance the way they can help their clients, beyond planning and investing. They tell us that doing the things we describe in this book fulfills their sense of meaning in their lives and practices. It provides the next step in professionalism and being able to help people in many different ways.

The idea of writing this book began on an airplane flight from the Northeast back to Los Angeles where we both live. We had just finished presenting a training session that our clients said was the best they had ever heard. We knew that we had very successfully presented information that was very effective in an advisor's business practice. However, we knew from our own experiences that there was something significantly greater we could do to help financial advisors.

We have both spent a lot of time involved in outside activities helping people in other aspects of their lives, beyond their financial needs. Because we both had many friends and contacts outside the financial area, we were frequently asked for personal help in issues that had nothing to do with our business. Helping solve someone's life problems was much more meaningful and fulfilling than making their finances right. Out of this thought came the very simple advice we give to financial advisors, *"service your clients first, and their money second."* Most Advisors are now readily buying into this concept. They just don't know specifically what we mean by serving their clients. This is the primary question we hope to answer. Not only what to do, but why it is important and why it improves an advisor's business.

This was the beginning of a year-long venture to see if the concept of strategically helping people could ethically and professionally become an appropriate and enhancing part of most financial advisors' practice. As we wrestled with the concept and its application, we found that in many cases it was a very natural thing that people do for each other. However, it often occurs through happenstance, and is limited. We have postulated that with a little work, it is something financial advisors can do on purpose for many of their clients' non-financial needs. We wondered if we could integrate what people do naturally and reactively into something they do purposely. We asked if advisors couldn't be much more effective and important to their clients' success if they spent as much time researching the best of the best in providing non-financial help for their clients as they did researching which firm was the best at managing money for their clients. We concluded that they can and should.

The problem we were facing was that we had boiled down all of our training material into 23 separate training modules and seldom ever had an opportunity to present more than three or four to any one group of advisors. It just seemed like our audiences were only getting part of the information we had accumulated over the past 35-plus years. They were getting far less than we had to offer and this bothered us. Somehow we didn't feel that over 70 years of our personal experience, and observing thousands of other successful people, would be as effective if diluted down into one-hour presentations.

We were looking for how we could pull everything together in a manner that could be effectively delivered to financial advisors. It is just not feasible to do it all in one presentation, and no one was willing to spend the time to do a series of sessions. In fact, the programs our clients asked us to participate in too often only allowed us one hour in a day-long series of "talking heads" presenting fragmented, unrelated hour-long sessions. We knew from our own experiences attending these types of serial presentations that these sessions could be as confusing as they were informative. We know from research of several psychologists that people attending these sessions seldom remember or put into practice more than seven percent of what they heard. Our own experience of attending management sessions and being bombarded with a stream of presenters sent us home more depressed than inspired and informed.

The most effective training we had ever conducted involved a three-day "boot camp" session. These included totally choreographed presentations allowing for participatory breakout sessions, and several months of follow-up reinforcement. Although we tried many times to get firms to make a similar time commitment, only one firm was willing to make that commitment. Everyone else would ask us to hit the highlights with a keynote address or occasionally put on a two-hour workshop.

We reluctantly concluded that the only way we could bring together a comprehensive body of work that would benefit our clients was to put the information into a book. Then, we would use our oral presentations to position and highlight information that could be supplemented by the rest of the information the book provides.

By the time we landed in Los Angeles, we had made a commitment to see if we were capable of organizing and writing such a book. We figured that our early experience on the East Coast, in the Midwest and the Northwest before arriving in California would allow us to shape a book that had a universal culture and geographic perspective. We obviously looked at putting much of the information together from our own experiences and perspective. But we also borrowed and utilized many other peoples' experiences, ideas and successes.

We spent a lot of time reviewing what our own experiences had taught us. We each had over 35 years of experience working in the securities industry, starting in the mid to late-1960s. We were struck by how much the industry is the same and yet how dramatically it has changed. The changes of technology, communication and the money involved are quite obvious.

The real differences are the changes that made today's profession as a financial advisor totally different than what we knew as young people in the industry. Many changes happened slowly and incrementally so it is not really very obvious that the industry is so very different and is changing at an increasing rate. There was no single change that had revolutionized the business; it has been a continual evolution of change. What became obvious to us was that to really understand the current financial advisory market, it was necessary to understand how the industry started and developed over a long period of time. We felt that the history was important to understanding the industry as we now find it. We were convinced that it was important to explore the multiple activities, events and changes that shaped the industry as we know it today. We felt that it would be necessary to carry the evolution concept through the book to provide the proper base to see that becoming a Life Advisor was just the next step in a process of long continual change.

Our own combined experiences had taken us through a variety of positions and responsibilities. We had been retail brokers, institutional brokers, product managers, marketing directors, specialists in using research, CEO and President of securities firms, and directors of trust departments and mutual funds. We had over 20 years experience managing retail, futures and institutional sales offices in several different parts of the country.

Each of us has served on more charity boards than we could remember and have over 20 years experi-

Introduction

ence teaching within the industry before we began our consulting practice. Richard has chaired and been on the curriculum committee for the Securities Industry Institute for over 15 years. We have both taught at the Securities Industry Institute at the Wharton School and heard hundreds of the top speakers in the industry there. We had worked for firms on both coasts and in many locations in between and experienced many different business cultures. Our own experience and backgrounds helped us have a broad perspective.

Our previous book, "Investment Survival," specifically focused on financial advisors and individuals using securities research, and taught us that bringing a lot of information together in a logical, pragmatic manner was very useful and needed in the industry. That book has now sold over 10,000 copies and been approved for continuing education for several different professional designations, including insurance, Certified Financial Planning, and CIMA, and has also been used for CPA and NASD continuing education.

When we started our consulting practice, the Quantum Leap Institute, our experiences were primarily with the big wirehouse and regional firm environments. We are now fortunate to work with many different firms and meet people in almost every state in the country. We began to examine what was happening in the independent practice and fee-only financial planning part of the business. We were exposed to people in almost every channel that work with finances, the big wirehouse firms, firms that focused on individuals in small towns, independent advisors, fee-only planners, banks and CPAs. We felt we had learned as much in our consulting practice as we had been able to teach others. When reviewing much of the information we use in our practice, it was obvious that a majority of it came from observing and working with hundreds of outstanding professionals in the industry. But the key to becoming a Life Advisor seemed to be absent, except by accident, in every channel.

This led us to subscribing to books and magazines about the industry and many other subjects. We bought and read over 100 books covering finance, advisor practice and related subjects. We thought we would find a book that had already been written that pulled together the fragments of the puzzle we were struggling with.

Four things happened with this binge of reading and interviewing. First, we had to buy more bookshelves to hold the library we were accumulating. Secondly, except for books specifically focused on investing, we found that most of the books dealing with developing and managing a business practice provided no background on the industry, and contained little about meeting clients' non-financial needs. Everything seemed to be focused on becoming a "wealth manager" on getting "high net worth" clients. These are apparently the new buzzwords in the industry. There was not much of a difference from what was being suggested by the traditional brokerage approach. The only change was adopting a new title and trying to service larger accounts.

Finally, to our surprise, one of the most useful sources of practical advice came from a psychologist, Dr. Robert Cialdini, and his book on influence, "Influence: The Psychology of Persuasion." As usual, after a couple thousand dollars invested in books and hundred of hours reading them, we found that Cialdini's book

Introduction

was the most useful and appropriate source of information and could be bought online at Amazon.com for about $13. It is the best investment we ever made.

Understanding the size of the market and how different financial instruments have been created or changed said a lot about how things have changed, and the new challenges and opportunities for both advisors and investors. We wanted to have specific information on what has happened to finance and business in the past quarter century. So we dove into the 2000 Census data, which was an adventure in itself. There is so much information and it is so interesting, that the information we found significant in this area ballooned from a few pages to several chapters. We condensed a great deal of it down to appropriate and useful observations. We had intended to put the 38 charts of supporting census data into an appendix for those who wanted to see the figures that back up the conclusions. Our editor convinced us that using the most relevant information in the appropriate parts of text worked better for readers.

We have also been told that most people will not be as fascinated with the detailed history data as we are. The charts will have to find another vehicle.

After studying the census data, we found there was a disconnect between the facts and what we believed. We are convinced that to be a functional Life Advisor, one needs to know what is really happening to the people we seek to provide services to. It is not only the financial services industry that has changed; every industry has changed. Knowing what has happened in other industries helps a financial advisor to understand the evolution that is happening in our entire economy.

Becoming a Life Advisor

We know that there is growing wealth in the country, but knowing whose income and wealth is growing and whose is not is very important. Our classic assumptions of the growth and declines of professions and job classifications over a couple of decades can be very different from the impression one can get from the evening news and the popular press. The media's consideration of the time frame for change is dramatically shorter than what we believe is needed to understand the changing employment demographics. It is easier to manage a practice if one can understand who is working, who will be working and what kind of jobs they will be working at over the life of most financial advisors' active years in the business. The census data lays out a most interesting set of changes we are experiencing, and we hope we have helped provide a needed understanding of the problems and opportunities for building a modern Life Advisor practice. Many times, changes in other industries significantly impacts peoples' personal lives. Financial advisors need to help clients in addition to addressing the management of their money.

A number of things became obvious when contemplating putting all of this information together in a book. Financial advisors are really quite different than people in most other professions. The investment process requires that advisors must be knowledgeable about almost all of the 125 industry classifications used by Standard & Poor's. In addition, advisors must not only understand the economics of the United States, but they must also understand economies worldwide and the significant impact of globalization. Finally, they must be informed and semi-objective about state and federal politics and how legislation is impacting everything we do. No one can be an expert on all industries and countries, but advisors do gain a reasonable perspective on a very wide range of issues. It is this broad knowledge of how things have evolved, even if vague, and the broad range of people who advisors deal with as clients, that provides them with a very unique opportunity to develop their practices and provide outstanding personal service to their clients.

We felt we needed to provide a comprehensive look at where we are today to understand a broad landscape of the requirements and opportunities available to advisors today and what will come next. We wanted to look at a practice of providing valued services beyond their financial profession in order to help their clients today and into the future.

While all industries have gone through many changes, nothing has changed more that the role of financial professionals who deal directly with the public. Clients' needs have changed as life expectancies have increased. Helping people in their 80s and 90s was once an exception and is now becoming more of the norm. Working with people in their 80s and 90s will be even more of an issue in the next 20 years. They are probably going to need more life advice than financial advice in their later years.

We found we even needed to learn a different way of communicating effectively with older people. There was a most interesting interview, "Talk Isn't Cheap," in Senior Market Advisor in 2001, with Dave Solie, the CEO of Second Opinion in Woodland Hills, California. Dave has been a friend we have admired for many years. In the article, he says, "Selling to seniors depends on how well you communicate with them." He says he became a facilitator for older people to communicate, not an obstacle. Dave goes on to say, "One of the biggest challenges is how you manage somebody when you have bad news." These messages are as likely to be about non-financial news as they are about financial news. You will need all of your skills as a Life Advisor as your clients grow much older. Details of Dave Solie's recently released book can be found on *http://www.dsolie.com*.

The economy has globalized. The number of people managing their own wealth and providing their own retirement plans requires planning, estate and tax services at levels that no one was providing 30 years ago. The old paradigm of working for a big company for your whole career and having them provide a guaranteed retirement income and health benefits in retirement is gone. The skills advisors need to succeed today are very different than what they were just five or 10 years ago. Their relationships with clients are very different and need to be understood.

Before landing in Los Angeles we related stories back and forth about advisors and others being of significant help to their clients with life issues that were totally outside of their financial life. Bringing this back to the idea of writing a book, we concluded that the opportunity for success was available to financial advisors by using current knowledge and building the right contacts to move beyond being a financial advisor to becoming a *Life Advisor*.

CHAPTER 1

Evolution of the Financial Services Industry

The Industry has Changed from Servicing
Wealthy Individuals to a Diversified
Financial Business

The United States financial services industry is a
product of historical forces. In order to understand current business practices and predict
changes that will impact the industry, it is instructive to
consider the social, political and economic factors that
have shaped the financial services industry in the last
century. Technological developments fueled a dramatic
shift, first from a primarily agricultural economy to a
manufacturing-based economy, then to a mostly service
sector economy. These economic changes encouraged a
steady movement of the population from rural to urban
and suburban environments, and led to increasing levels
of education and prosperity. These economic, technological and social forces, coupled with government regu-

lations and reforms, helped shape the modern financial services industry.

Enduring Habits

Many business laws, rules and customs were established long ago, and are better understood if we comprehend why they were first instituted. Business conventions that today may appear arcane, irrational or inefficient are often legacies of systems that were established at one time for legitimate purposes. Circumstances change, while systems live on. We become comfortable with old ways of doing things and are sometimes reluctant to change. It can be hard to admit that the procedures and customs that have governed our lives are no longer relevant.

The story of the baked ham and the oven illustrates how habits and conventions can sometimes continue when they no longer serve a purpose. One holiday, an engineer was watching his wife prepare a baked ham for dinner. Before putting the ham in the oven, his wife sliced both ends off the ham. The curious engineer asked his wife why she cut the ends off the ham. She said it was the way her mother taught her to bake hams. Being an inquisitive engineer, he wanted to know the practical reason for cutting the ends off the ham. He called her mother, who said she didn't know the reason; it was the way her mother taught her to bake hams. The grandmother was still alive, so he called her. The grandmother at last supplied the very logical answer. She told him she had a very small oven and had to cut the ends off to get the ham to fit inside.

Many of today's business practices are like cutting

the ends off the ham — we accept conventions that appear not to make sense because they were established for legitimate reasons that are no longer relevant. The New York Stock Exchange specialist system, for example, does not seem to have a purpose in today's electronic exchanges, but when the job of the specialist originated in 1872, there was a need for a new system of continuous trading. Prior to the establishment of the specialist, each stock had a set time during which it could be traded. Under the new system, brokers would deal in a specific stock at one location on the floor of the exchange, so they could always be found. Eventually, the role of these brokers evolved into that of the specialist.

Sometimes legacy systems are codified in laws, regulations and statutes that may continue long past their usefulness. Legislators are so busy passing new laws in response to new crimes that there is little time to expunge antiquated laws. In the past, people sometimes did things that were perhaps not completely honest or fair, but were not yet illegal. Lawmakers are always playing catch-up, struggling to create statutes that take time to legislate and implement.

When laws are passed and are not effective or not in the public's best interest, people find ways that are not yet illegal to continue acting dishonestly or unfairly. To correct these abuses, more laws are passed. Sometimes, the behavior the laws were meant to abolish no longer occurs, but the laws are still on the books and sometimes are still being enforced. Statutes established in the early part of the century that govern conflicts between automobiles and horses, for example, can still be found in many older municipalities.

The Early 20th Century: 1900-1916

In the early 20th century, the country was introduced to the automobile. Few people at that time could envision the changes this single technological advancement would bring to every industry. The automobile had a dramatic impact on travel, transportation, where people lived and every aspect of American business and life.

The automobile first had an impact on American business when it was adapted to farming. Trucks and tractors helped improve yields, reduce the labor needed to plant and harvest crops, and increased the range agricultural products could be transported. People didn't have to be located near farms to ensure a supply of food or jobs, and were free to move about the country, settling in cities, improving their education for professional careers, or seeking higher-wage employment in new industrial plants and factories. Farm employment at the turn of the century represented about 30 percent of the population. Today, only about one percent of the U.S. workforce is employed in farming, producing all of the food products for the rest of the country and many other parts of the world.

Improvements in transportation also facilitated centralized production of manufactured goods, while advancements in machine technology and electrical systems made industrial manufacturing possible. The early part of the century saw a significant movement of people from agriculture to manufacturing, service and professional sectors, a trend that has continued to this day. Jobs were increasingly in the factories, which were located near transportation hubs in the cities, so that's where people went to look for work.

Evolution of the Financial Services Industry

Industrial companies required capital to build manufacturing and power plants, energy resources and transportation systems. The securities markets were developed to provide the money. The markets enabled capital to react more quickly, and provided new opportunities for promising entrepreneurs to raise money.

Wealth in the country shifted as well, from land ownership to ownership of manufacturing, transportation and energy resources. The industrial ownership model, facilitated by the securities industry, was vastly more flexible, liquid, and diversified than the agricultural system of ownership. While land ownership often remained in a single family for generations, ownership of industrial assets was spread among potentially tens of thousands of investors and rapidly changed hands as shares were traded in the securities markets.

Though securities markets enabled more people to invest in companies, a relatively small group of very rich people had near monopoly control of many industries. While they may not have directly owned all the assets of companies working in a particular industry, they frequently used interlocking trusts and boards of directors to control many of the companies. Their actions had a significant impact on prices, working conditions, wages and the entire financial operation of the country. The free market did not work well when all the power was in the hands of a few, very rich people.

Partly due to this concentrated ownership, the government was not able to stabilize the economy. Private bankers such as J.P. Morgan exerted much greater influence on the country's finances than the government. As a result, stock markets were much more volatile than they are today. Three times in the early part of the century, the Dow Jones averages fell by 30 to 50 percent, though by 1917 the stock market had tripled overall from its lowest point in 1904.

In 1901, an anarchist assassinated President William McKinley. Theodore Roosevelt became president, and a new age of federal activism began. With Roosevelt in the White House, the government exerted much more control over the U.S. economy. Roosevelt served until 1909 and aggressively enforced anti-trust laws throughout his time in office. Roosevelt led the government to attack the interlocking trust system, and for the first time, lawsuits were filed to enforce the Sherman Anti-Trust Act. Lawsuits were filed to break up railroad trusts, and Roosevelt is credited with dismantling the oil monopoly when the federal government sued the Standard Oil Company, which was fined $29 million.

The market panicked after the Standard Oil decision, and there was a run on banks as depositors withdrew their assets. The Mercantile Bank, the Knickerbocker Trust Company, and other financial institutions were rumored to be insolvent. United Copper stock dropped from 53 to 10 in one day. New York City could not find buyers for its bonds. The United States Treasury put $25 million into the banks to stave off their closing, but it was insufficient. Bank closings seemed inevitable until J.P. Morgan and some other New York bankers stepped in to provide enough liquid capital for the banks to regain the public's trust.

President Roosevelt was also more active than his predecessors in foreign policy, believing a firm hand would stabilize international politics as well as the American economy. Under his leadership, the United States Navy developed into one of the most powerful in the world. Roosevelt also helped negotiate the end of the Russo-Japanese War, for which he won the Nobel Peace Prize.

After Roosevelt left office, he became disillusioned with his handpicked successor, Howard Taft. Roosevelt formed the independent Bull Moose Party, but failed in his 1912 run for the presidency, although his participation in the election split the Republican Party and enabled Woodrow Wilson to be elected the first democratic president of the 20th century.

Roosevelt's activist legacy lived on after his presidency. In 1913, the Federal Reserve Act was passed, creating the Federal Reserve Board to help regulate the nation's currency. In 1914, the Clayton Anti-Trust Act was passed to regulate interlocking directorates of corporations.

World War I to the Stock Market Crash: 1917-1929

World War I marked the beginning of a major period of growth in the American economy. The production of armaments and supplies for "The Great War" accelerated the transition to a manufacturing economy. Capital was invested in new plants and equipment. A growing workforce, increasingly displaced from a farming industry that had lost jobs, flocked to the cities in search of factory work. The nation's transportation infrastructure was strengthened to help move bullets, bombs and butter to soldiers in Europe. The war was hard for the soldiers, but it was good for business back home.

After the war, the League of Nations was established, and many people believed that the first world war would be "the war to end all wars." While Europe recovered and rebuilt, America entered a period of growth and optimism. The country had proven itself on the battlefield, side by side with the great European nations, but unlike much of Europe, was left relatively unscathed after the war. The isolationism that was popular after the Spanish-American War at the turn of the century, when many politicians feared the United States would become an empire, had been replaced with a new feeling of international strength, responsibility and engagement.

The nation opened its doors to international exchange and commerce, and the economy flourished as a result, impacting every aspect of American life and culture. A mostly agrarian society governed on principles of restraint and stewardship plunged into a period of decadent hedonism and unimaginable wealth for business tycoons.

The "Roaring '20s" pushed the American securities markets into the modern age. The stock market soared as the economy grew, and in an age when there was virtually no government regulation, speculators gambled on the markets and frequently got rich beyond their imagining. More people were drawn to speculate in the markets, borrowing heavily to buy stocks. A few people advised caution, but most investors stayed at the party until the very end. The great crash would dramatically change the country, bringing a new period of restraint, responsibility and regulation.

Great Depression through the End of World War II: 1929-1945

The wild exuberance leading up to the stock market crash was matched in severity by the crippling Depression that gripped the country in its wake. Economists reassessed many of their most cherished theories, including those supporting an unregulated free market, which had been seen by many as a perfect, unerring and universally beneficial system. Prior to the crash, major corporations and the financial service industry operated with little or no regulation, and the country was seen to prosper as a result. The market crash and economic depression changed not only the economy, but also people's attitudes toward government regulation. The federal government passed legislation and implemented reforms that shaped the financial industry. Many of the regulatory changes of the 1930s are still the basis for most market regulation.

The Dow Jones Industrial average sank 339.85 points from 1929 to 1932, from a high of 381.17 in 1929 to a low of 41.22 in 1932, wiping out 89 percent of the value of its stocks. Many hard-working Americans lost everything they owned. Leading up to the crash, many investors had borrowed heavily against their stocks in order to buy more stocks. Some borrowed up to 90 percent of the value of their portfolio. After the market decline, these heavily-leveraged investors lost all their equity. Their entire portfolio had to be sold, accelerating the market's downward spiral. Their portfolios eliminated, their savings lost in bank failures, their businesses bankrupt and their homes repossessed, millions of Americans were left destitute. Those left with a job that provided only enough to feed their families were considered lucky.

The streets were full of people looking for handouts. The soup kitchens were overflowing and bread lines ran for blocks. Distraught fathers left their families, traveling the country looking for work of any kind, and many never returned. Children suffered malnutrition, hunger, and even starvation to an extent that had never been seen in the nation's history. The birth rate dropped, and infant mortality rose.

Presidents Harding and Coolidge had staunchly defended business interests, placed little restraint on the free market, and had encouraged the speculation that led to the stock market boom in the 1920s, and the subsequent market crash that began in 1929. Americans had seen the markets generate extraordinary wealth, but they had also seen them run wildly off course, causing wealth to evaporate seemingly overnight. Many people who had formerly championed the free market came to believe the system desperately needed reform. Unfortunately, the first efforts at reform proved disastrous.

The first act of Congress in 1930 was to pass the Smoot–Hawley Tariff, which raised international tariffs to historically high levels. American farmers were being hurt by foreign agricultural imports made cheap by massive agricultural overproduction in Europe. Originally intended to increase protections for domestic farmers, the Smoot–Hawley Tariff restricted trade, and prolonged the country's economic malaise.

The federal government did not provide many social services, relief efforts, or jobs programs at the time. Social services were mostly left to state agencies and religious charities. Drained of resources by the plunging economy, most states had little ability to deal with the enormous problems facing them. President Hoover implemented some relief programs and public works projects, but his efforts were limited. Failing to significantly improve the economy or relieve Americans' suffering, Hoover lost the 1932 election to Franklin Roosevelt.

Franklin Roosevelt was elected on the promise that he would make changes to help the economy. Disagreements between President Roosevelt and Congress prevented some of the more dramatic changes that were proposed at the time, but a great deal of regulatory legislation was passed that created the foundation of today's financial markets.

Many banks and securities firms declared bankruptcy after the 1929 market crash. The public lost confidence in the nation's financial institutions. Very few people continued to invest in equities. Few people had excess money to invest, and many believed equity investment of any kind to be dangerous speculation. People wanted safe investments first and foremost, and turned to banks, and savings and loan companies, to provide them. Saving accounts became the primary instrument people used to safeguard their excess money, if they trusted banks at all.

The financial industry at this time was comprised of small consumer banks and larger central commercial banks. The central banks took deposits and lent money to individuals and corporations, and were also the investment banks of the day, performing initial public offerings, mergers and retail brokerage services. The J.P. Morgan Bank, for example, was prominent in both commercial and investment banking.

To address some of the abuses and speculation that led up to the crash, Congress passed the Glass-Steagall Act in 1933, separating commercial and investment functions. J.P. Morgan became a strictly commercial bank, while Morgan Stanley was created to continue as an investment bank and broker. Glass-Steagall had no impact on firms that were primarily investment banks or brokers, such as Goldman Sachs, Lehman Brothers, Drexel Harriman, Edward Jones or A.G. Edwards, although it prohibited them from buying or becoming commercial banks.

To prevent banks from competing for deposits by paying ever-higher interest rates, which would have required very high lending rates, rules were passed setting the maximum interest rates banks could pay on deposits. To prevent brokerage firms from competing by deeply discounting commissions, which would further weaken their financial stability, minimum commission rates were set for securities firms. These regulations were adjusted over time, but remained largely unchanged for decades.

The Securities Act of 1933 forced greater disclosure in the industry, while the Securities Exchange Act of 1934 regulated the trading exchanges. These statutes contributed to a more open and fair market, and with few changes, are the same basic laws that regulate the industry today, though additional rules have been added to address abusive practices that periodically surfaced.

Only a handful of mutual funds were formed during the 1920s. Mutual funds represented only $140 million by the end of 1929. Mutual fund investing did not start to grow again until after securities legislation was passed from 1933 through 1940. The Revenue Act of 1936 legislated the tax treatment for mutual funds and their shareholders, while the Investment Company Act of 1940 established the structure and regulatory framework for the modern mutual fund industry. Investor confidence was bolstered by the protections afforded by these new regulations, and assets invested in mutual funds increased.

The gold standard, which tied the U.S. currency to the value of the gold held in the U.S. Treasury, was determined by many in the government to be restricting free trade and hindering the economy, though many conservative bankers considered it to be an essential hedge against inflation. In an effort to help get the economy moving again, the gold standard was dropped in 1933. The role the elimination of the gold standard played in the Great Depression is debatable, but the economy was very slow to recover in the 1930s. Few houses were built during this period, manufacturing almost came to a halt, and the financial industry was barely surviving.

World War II began in Europe in 1939. While the United States did not enter the war immediately, the country supplied the Allies with war materials and other exports. The economy accelerated as a result, and helped the country recover from the long Depression that began 10 years earlier.

In 1941, the bombing of Pearl Harbor pushed the United States into the war. Wartime production of armaments and equipment transformed the economy. Nearly all manufacturing was converted to supporting the war. Factories ran full time to produce military goods. Many women joined the workforce for the first time, filling factory jobs as 16 million men and women joined the military. The federal government implemented price fixing and rationing of materials, food and fuel needed to supply the war effort. To pay for the war and prevent profiteering, the top income tax rate was raised to 94 percent, by far the highest since the 25 percent rate was implemented in 1926.

Prior to the war, fresh fruits and vegetables were primarily seasonal. The rest of the year, people ate canned or frozen produce. Self-sufficiency was the norm as a lack of timely, efficient and affordable shipping and transportation, along with federal trade tariffs, made international trade prohibitively expensive for most people. The Bretton Woods Agreement in 1944 helped increase international trade and investment. Foreseeing the end of the war, delegates from all 44 Allied nations gathered in the New Hampshire town of Bretton Woods for the United Nations Monetary and Financial Conference in order to work out an international agreement that would support post-war reconstruction. The Bretton Woods Agreement established the International Monetary Fund and the International Bank for Reconstruction and Development, which assisted in the reconstruction and development of economies hurt by the war, and helped promote loans, private foreign investment, and the balanced growth of international trade.

The war ended September 2, 1945. As incomes rose and trade barriers decreased, more international goods came to the United States. The public's taste had changed as well, as millions of people in the military, stationed in other countries, were exposed to foods and merchandise from all over the world. Though the economy took several years to retool and regain momentum, post-war America was a very different place than the country that had experienced the Great Depression.

Evolution of the Financial Services Industry

The Post-War Period: 1945-1959

A post-war recession began in 1946 as manufacturers switched from making war goods to producing consumer goods. The stock market had risen during the war to a DOW level of 212, well above 42.84, the low experienced after the 1929 crash, but still more than 168 points below the peak of 1929. After the war, the DOW sank 27 percent to 167.

The economy improved dramatically after the post-war recession, and the securities markets rebounded to produce one of the longest and largest bull markets of the century. New factories were built and more people moved to cities in search of jobs. The population also moved westward. The West Coast was now familiar to many more people, as much of the country's wartime aircraft manufacturing had been on the West Coast, and troops had moved through the area on their way to fight the war in the Pacific. Many people who had seen the West Coast decided to relocate there after the war.

Few cars were built during the 1930s and '40s as companies focused on wartime production, or struggled to convert factories back to peacetime production after the war. Car companies did not begin producing significant numbers of cars until 1951. From this point on, the automotive industry was a major driver of the economy.

In the early 1950s, the economy suffered from inflation as demand for consumer products increased. Fearing the boom-and-bust cycles of the 1920s and 1930s, the federal government sought ways to accommodate a growing economy while controlling its excesses. In 1951, the government approved a U.S. Treasury-Federal Reserve Accord to help control interest rates and inflation.

In 1952, newly powerful labor unions were granted wage increases in the steel industry, and as a result, steel companies planned to significantly raise prices. The federal government, fearing excessive inflation, seized the steel mills in an attempt to control prices. The government had come a long way from the laissez faire days of the 1920s. Although the mills were quickly returned to the operating companies when an agreement was reached on pricing, the government had shown itself willing to intervene in the economy in ways it never had before.

Growing international trade was a noticeable feature of the post-war economy. Prior to the war, protectionist policies in many countries limited international trade. Many countries saw inexpensive goods from other parts of the world as a threat to their economies, unless the goods in question were not produced within their borders. Even then, many who advocated protectionist statutes preferred to go without rather than embrace international trade.

After the war, many countries saw the benefits of international trade. Tariffs and other impediments to trade were reduced or eliminated. The General Agreement on Tariffs and Trade (GATT) was first signed by many industrial nations in 1947 to encourage and regulate international trade. A new global economy was emerging.

The United States was especially aggressive in international trade as the country could no longer produce enough oil to inexpensively meet its growing demand. Oil reserves that dwarfed America's had been discovered in the Middle East, and the nation sought to reduce trade barriers to keep cheap oil flowing to the United States With lower tariffs and more efficient means of transportation, U.S. manufacturers were also able to sell more goods and services overseas.

During the war, the United States had to greatly expand and improve its ship and airplane manufacturing capabilities. Many of the new designs developed during the war made for more efficient, lower-cost international transportation, which made goods from other countries increasingly affordable and available. The war had also broken down many cultural and nationalist attitudes. Consumers were increasingly open to foreign products.

As the Cold War developed in the 1950s, it was also in our nation's interest to strengthen ties with the economies of Germany and Japan. Though Germany and Japan needed to repair and replace transportation infrastructures and manufacturing facilities destroyed during the war, both countries were recognized as having well-educated, industrious and technologically-savvy populations. The Marshall Plan proved to be a wise investment as reconstruction funds poured into Germany and Japan, creating new factories and skilled labor forces that produced inexpensive goods that could be exported to the United States.

Farming and manufacturing productivity in the United States also made domestic goods more widely available and affordable. People had more spending money after the war, as wages increased more rapidly in the United States than in much of the rest of the world. As incomes increased, consumption and retail purchasing increased. The service sector came into its own after the war. People ate out more, and spent more money on leisure activities. More people also needed accounting, legal and other professional services.

Becoming a Life Advisor

The 1950s also saw major changes in the way people worked, and the places they lived. Many people had migrated from the South during the war to find jobs in the cities. Not only manufacturing, but also most retail and office work was concentrated in city centers at the end of the war. The increase in the number of automobiles, and the many new roads and highways provided by the federal government's National Highway Defense Act made commuting more efficient. People moved away from the cities, to suburban enclaves outside urban areas. Retail, commercial, professional and manufacturing businesses also moved out of the cities. The new suburban communities tended to be more segregated by income and race than the cities. Wealth and resources concentrated outside urban areas, contributing to the decline of city centers experienced in the latter half of the 20th century.

As the economy grew in the 1950s, more people looked for ways to invest their savings. The securities industry grew in response to a new wave of investors. New financial products and services were introduced, and the way industry professionals worked with their clients changed dramatically.

As the economy grew, company earnings increased. Investors saw prices of some stocks going up much faster than their income from dividends. Corporate executives said they could provide higher returns for investors by keeping the money in the company and reinvesting it, or buying other companies, rather than distributing income in the form of dividends. Dividends were taxed at current income rates, but investors could benefit from stock appreciation without paying taxes until the stocks were sold. Investors became more willing to accept lower dividend yields and lower interest rates on bonds in exchange for price appreciation and total return from stock investments. This was a dramatic and permanent change for investors, and represented the real beginning of the securities markets as we know them today. Securities firms such as Merrill Lynch, Bache, Dean Witter and Goodbody opened offices across the nation and launched programs to educate the public on investing. For the first time, Wall Street was coming to Main Street.

Mutual funds became much more popular during the 1950s. It was not until 1951 that the number of mutual funds surpassed 100, and the number of shareholder accounts exceeded one million. By 1954, purchases of mutual funds exceeded those of corporate stock. In 1954, the first U.S.-based international mutual fund was introduced. By 1961, the first tax-free investment trust was offered.

Retirement and pension plans also increased after the war. A significant portion of the growth in the number of investors in the 1950s was due to the increase in employee retirement programs, and the change from defined benefit plans to defined contribution plans. Under defined benefit plans, companies guaranteed retirement benefits. Company actuaries determined how much money was needed in the retirement trust to provide benefits. Money in the trust was generated by company contributions and the earnings gained on the trust's invested assets. The higher the earnings on existing assets, the less money the company had to contribute. As total returns on stocks were much higher than those earned from the interest on bonds, corporate, state and municipal pension funds and retirement plans invested more of their assets in the stock market, which had previously been considered too risky for pensions and retirement funds.

Individuals also invested more of their money in the stock market, and had increasing control over their retirement plan investments, as retirement accounts changed from defined benefit plans to defined contribution plans, in which companies put money in trusts that were under the control of individual investors. The change from defined benefit plans to defined contribution plans was accelerated by the federal government, which created programs in which investors were given favorable tax treatment for their retirement accounts. The introduction of Individual Retirement Accounts (IRAs), employee stock purchase plans, and 401(k) retirement plans were responsible for much of the increases in individual equity ownership.

As more individuals owned stocks, the need for investment information and counseling grew commensurately. To satisfy the demand, many securities firms expanded their research departments and started issuing reports on many more companies.

The increase in individual investments in the stock market indicated a general change in the attitudes of many Americans toward their economic prospects. Prior to the war, many people felt they were destined to work in the same jobs their parents had. After the war, many veterans used the GI Bill to go to school and buy their first homes. There was a palpable optimism in the country. The baby boom was indicative of people's hopes for the future. Having grown up in the Great Depression, many parents wanted their children to have better lives than they had. Material success was a significant priority, and many people saw investing in the markets as a good way to increase their prosperity.

Changing Times: 1960-1979

The American economy, society, culture, business practices and investment markets all changed dramatically in the 1960s and 1970s. Social and demographic forces drove many of the changes. Baby boomers conceived after World War II entered schools and universities in record numbers. Parents who had been through the Great Depression and World War II were determined their children get the education many of them had not.

Political, technological and social changes in the 1960s and '70s led to many family and personal behaviors we take for granted today, including a dramatic change in the assumed role of women in the family and workplace. The introduction of birth control pills allowed increasing numbers of women to postpone child bearing, complete their college education, and enter the workforce. A greater percentage of women joined the workforce in the 1960s and '70s than at any time in American history. The large numbers of women and baby boomers entering the workforce led to a significant increased demand for new jobs for the increase in job seekers.

The 1960s were a time of political upheaval. Americans were consumed with the Cold War. Nuclear missiles were built and stockpiled by the United States and the Soviet Union. Fidel Castro came to power in Cuba, which became the only communist government in the Western Hemisphere. The United States erected trade barriers and restrictions on Cuba that are still in place today. In 1961, the United States supported a failed attempt to invade Cuba at the Bay of Pigs. When Soviet missile shipments to Cuba were confirmed in 1962, the Kennedy administration insisted the missiles be removed, in what has since become known as "The Cuban Missile Crisis."

President Kennedy was assassinated in Dallas, Texas in 1963. Lyndon Johnson became president, and was re-elected in a landslide. The Johnson administration was noted for its efforts to address domestic problems, including trying to satisfy the demand for more jobs and addressing poverty levels. Johnson's "War on Poverty" expanded many of the social programs created by Franklin Roosevelt, and created new programs to help those in need.

The civil rights movement led to violence-laden freedom marches, and police and white backlashes in many states, and culminated in new civil rights legislation, including the Civil Rights Act and the Voting Rights Act, both passed in 1964. School desegregation, mandated by the Supreme Court's Brown vs. the Board of Education decision in 1954, was resisted in several Southern states, causing President Kennedy to use the National Guard to enforce the statute.

The United States entered the Vietnam War in 1965. The war consumed and divided the nation for a decade, and had a major impact on the country's culture and economy. The war sapped the nation's economic strength, and along with the oil embargo, caused persistently high rates of inflation in the 1970s. Commodity prices —particularly oil — soared, and wage increases of 10 percent annually were commonplace. The impact on every industry was reflected in the stock market. The

DOW hit a new high of 1,000 in 1966, and declined by almost 50 percent by 1974.

High inflation and slow economic growth in the 1970s were labeled "stagflation." Government policies were adopted to fight inflation, but to little effect. President Nixon imposed price controls. President Ford implemented a public program called WIN (Whip Inflation Now) to urge the public to help curb inflation. None of these policies were effective in combating the inflation of the 1970s.

U.S. manufacturing declined precipitously in the 1960s and '70s. As wages increased, the difference in labor costs between the United States and other countries spurred companies to move manufacturing facilities overseas. Almost all home appliances and electronic goods had been manufactured in the United States during the 1950s. American brand names such as RCA, Zenith, Motorola and Sunbeam dominated the market. In the 1960s and '70s, imported products appeared at much lower prices. American manufacturers still controlled the market for quality items, but were not competitive for lower-priced goods. Household and electronic products were increasingly designed in the United States and manufactured elsewhere. Foreign companies steadily improved the quality of their goods, while keeping prices low. Virtually no appliances or electronic products are manufactured in the United States today.

Several new industries emerged in the 1960s and '70s. The pharmaceutical industry gained strength as new drugs were developed and introduced. The technology industry went from being a novelty to a major commercial industry. IBM was the dominant computer company, but new companies like Wang and Digital Equipment Corporation gained market share. Xerox was revolutionizing the copy business.

Securities markets evolved in the 1970s after operating much the same way for previous decades. Securities brokerage fees were deregulated in May 1975. Previously, the Securities and Exchange Commission had regulated securities transactions. The commission rate had been fixed in the 1930s because of low trading volume and the fear that rate competition would drive securities firms into bankruptcy and diminish the viability of a competitive auction market.

Many industries were seriously impacted by high interest rates and price increases in materials and labor. Problems in the economy were reflected in the bear market in secondary stocks. Smaller companies were suffering, though the secondary stock decline did not have much impact on the Dow Jones Average or the Standard and Poor's index. Institutional investors, avoiding secondary stocks, focused on very large growth stocks. By 1972, these stocks were commonly referred to as the "Nifty Fifty." Common wisdom at the time was to buy large, high-growth stocks and hold them forever.

At the time, outstanding bonds carried low interest rates. The rates were set at the time the bonds were issued. Some of the long-term bonds issued over the previous 30 years had coupon rates as low as 2.5 percent. As market interest rates rose, the market value of these outstanding bonds declined. Interest rates on outstanding bonds were well below the level of yearly inflation, giving investors a negative net return after taxes and inflation. Large corporate pension funds found the low bond rates were no longer sufficient to meet their retirement fund obligations. The value of bond portfolios dropped dramatically.

Having witnessed the sharp rise in stock prices, trustees changed their investment policies, raising their equity allocation to as high as 80 percent of their total portfolio assets. To diversify their equity holdings, they hired bank trust departments to mange their equity portfolios. Most of the banks invested in the same Nifty Fifty stocks, so there was in fact very little diversity. The influx of assets into Nifty Fifty stocks caused their prices to escalate, leading to a price bubble and an eventual collapse in stock prices.

The market decline lasted from 1973 to 1974, causing the broad indexes and individual stocks to decline by nearly 50 percent. The Nifty Fifty stocks that had propped up the market in the early '70s took a particularly sever beating. With the decline of the Nifty Fifty stocks, and the generally poor showing of secondary stocks, there was nowhere for investors to go. As both individual and institutional investors pulled back from the markets, trading volume declined. The state of Michigan retirement funds, for example, did not execute one transaction in their several billion dollar stock portfolio in an 18-month period.

Transaction commissions at the time were the primary income for both brokerage firms and their advisors. Their earnings dropped significantly. Many of the new advisors that had been hired in the previous decade did not have a big enough client base to support them. It is estimated that half of all stock advisors working for the wirehouses left the business in the mid-1970s.

Becoming a Life Advisor

After the Watergate investigation and facing impeachment, Richard Nixon resigned from office in 1974, becoming the first president in the history of the United States to resign. Gerald Ford, who had been appointed and confirmed as the new vice president after Spiro Agnew's resignation, became the 38th president of the United States and the first man to ascend to the presidency who had not been elected vice president.

Though the Vietnam War ended in 1975, and social unrest had largely abated by the end of the decade, inflation persisted. President Carter appointed Paul Volker as chairman of the Federal Reserve Board in 1979. Volker led the Fed to increase interest rates and reserve requirements to the highest levels in decades, contributing to a severe recession in the U.S. economy. Short-term rates were raised to over 20 percent. Every industry was affected. Home building came to a halt. Consumer finance and corporate investment were severely impacted. These problems were reflected in the securities markets. Stocks declined and investors flocked to long-term bonds.

Retirement plans spurred the growth of mutual funds in the 1960s and '70s. Mutual funds became the primary investment choice for most defined contribution retirement plans. In 1962, the Self-Employment Individuals Tax Retirement Act created tax-favored saving plans (Keogh plans) for self-employed individuals. In 1974, the government passed the Employee Retirement Income Security Act (ERISA), which created Individual Retirement Accounts (IRAs) for workers not covered by employer retirement plans, even if they were not self-employed.

Evolution of the Financial Services Industry

Money market mutual funds were introduced in 1971, paying much higher interest rates than checking and savings accounts, which caused a dramatic shift of assets from bank deposits and savings accounts to money market funds, leading to significant changes in the industry and the introduction of important new products.

Congress encouraged the growth of mutual funds by passing The Revenue Act of 1978, which permitted the creation of 401(k) retirement plans and Simplified Employer Pensions (SEPs). The growth of mutual funds, accelerated by the ongoing shift from fixed benefit to fixed contribution retirements plans, led to significantly more assets invested in the stock market.

Even with the increasing interest in the markets, total transaction volume on the New York Stock Exchange was still averaging well below 10 millions shares a day in the early 1970s. When volume did increase, the use of paper certificates to record the transfer of ownership slowed the system. Transfer delays got so bad, the markets had to shorten trading hours and close the market on Wednesdays to catch up on paperwork.

The most significant trend in the securities industry during the 1960s and '70s was the proliferation of new products, and in some cases, whole new industries. New insurance policies and annuities, stock and bond derivatives, mortgage trusts, energy and real estate partnerships, and a host of other financial products provided unlimited permutations for investment. Very few clients really understood most of these complex investments, and in some cases, even the advisors and investment bankers didn't understand them as well as they should have. Nevertheless, it was an exciting, dynamic time for the securities industry.

In the 1950s, only insurance agents sold insurance policies. Many times, insurance agents were "captive," which meant they only represented one sponsoring company. Large companies like New York Life, Metropolitan Life, Northwestern Mutual, and Equitable dominated the industry. Many of these were "mutual companies" owned by their policyholders, as opposed to stock companies, which are publicly traded and can pit the company's interests against the policyholders.' Most mutual companies have now converted to stock companies.

Increasing use of derivative products in the 1970s helped shape the modern securities industry, facilitating many attractive new financial products. Large financial commitments could be made using options, futures, and options on futures without ever trading the underlying bond, stock or currency. Derivatives were frequently used for pure speculation on individual stocks, or by institutions to diminish the risk of a large inventory of stocks or bonds. If an equity or bond portfolio manager believed stock prices would move significantly in either direction, for example, they could protect their investments by executing an option contract. By not having to trade the underlying security, derivatives enabled a portfolio manager to avoid contributing to large price changes of the stocks, and avoid transaction costs that are greater than the cost of the derivatives contract. Derivatives were also used by trading desks to process large trades without actually buying or selling the stock. The trader would buy or sell options, for example, and then liquidate the option position when they were able to trade the actual security. In this manner, derivatives increased liquidity in both equity and fixed income markets.

The highly-leveraged nature of derivatives, however, could have unexpected repercussions for the investor. Using derivatives, a small amount of money can control very large underlying securities positions. Returns can be significant, providing everything works out according to plan. When things don't happen as anticipated, losses can be astronomical, as many firms and clients have sadly found out. Derivatives should be handled with care, and are not advisable for clients who cannot tolerate high risk.

Derivatives have had a tremendous impact on world trade and financial institutions. World trade is made efficient by futures contracts that allow parties to hedge shifts in currency prices. An international contract can be agreed to at a set price because each party can use futures contracts to make sure a change in currency prices will not impact the transaction. As late as the 1970s, economic models lacked a way to quantify expectations of future interest rates. Financial futures provided this data.

Options on securities were modeled after the options used in real estate. It has long been a practice for a specific buyer of real estate to pay a fee to a specific seller to have the option to purchase a property at a set price with a set date of expiration. Depending on how the contract was written, the owner of the option could sometimes sell the option to another party.

Options were initially contracts to buy or sell a specific security at a specific price on a specific date. The contracts were negotiated between two parties with any unique conditions agreed to by both parties. These are referred to as European options. There were many benefits to buying or selling options, but trying to match buyers and sellers was a problem. The options market at the time was dominated by large contracts specifically tailored to each party's needs.

Option trading was formalized with the creation of the Chicago Board Options Exchange (CBOE) in 1973. Prior to the founding of the CBOE, options contracts were specifically structured and backed by the parties involved. On April 26, the first day of trading, 911 contracts traded on 16 original underlying stocks. In 1975, the Options Clearing Corporation (OCC) was formed, and would eventually become the largest options clearing organization in the world. In 1977, "put" options were introduced. Options traded on the CBOE are backed by the clearing organization, not the individuals holding the contracts.

The largest volume of futures contracts are traded on the Chicago Mercantile Exchange (CME). The Merc, as it was originally known, was created in 1898 and at first only traded commodity contracts on agricultural goods, like cattle and grains. The ability to trade contracts that set future prices allowed farmers and ranchers to know what price they could get at harvest, and producers to know what they would have to pay. Speculators provided the liquidity to help the market work. Today, futures are traded on many markets around the world. The CME now has four major product areas: interest rates, stock indexes, foreign exchanges, and agricultural commodities. The value of agricultural contracts is now dwarfed by the trade in financial contracts. Another type of derivative product that provided significant benefits for investors was the new variable annuity contracts introduced in the late 1970s. Variable annuity contracts were designed for retirement investments, and appealed to more aggressive investors who also wanted the benefits of annuity tax deferral. Variable annuities were similar to mutual funds, as they were based on an underlying equity portfolio and were managed by professional money managers, but allowed for the transfer of funds between portfolios without tax consequences until money is withdrawn from the contract.

As policyholders demanded higher-return insurance products, insurance companies began to offer annuities, whose values were based on their underlying investments. Annuity products still carried an element of insurance because they provided some modest death benefits. Because people buying annuities were concerned about risk, however, insurance companies charged extra fees to guarantee the death benefit would be no less than the original amount invested, plus a set rate of increases that in most cases were similar to the interest on conservative fixed income investments.

Insurance companies created many new products in the 1960s and 1970s. Initially, life insurance policies were just that, policies to provide money to fulfill one's financial obligations if death arrived early. Policies basically came in two styles: term life and whole life. Term life had premiums that were fixed for the short term but increased as the policyholder grew older. There was no cash built up, and no residual value to the policy; it was purely premature death protection. The policy stayed in force as long as the buyer was current on their premium payments. Early term insurance policies were called industrial insurance and premiums were frequently collected in cash each month by the insurance agent.

Whole-life policies had fixed lifetime premiums or sometimes fixed premiums for a specified number of years. The policy accrued a cash value that the policyholder could borrow against, so whole life policies were generally more expensive than term policies. Whole life policies served as both premature death protection and conservative investment vehicles. The insurance company was required to maintain reserve investments to guarantee the money would be there when its policies matured.

The insurance industry introduced universal life policies in the late 1960s. Universal life policies provided for the insurance companies to invest a portion of the premiums, and the policies were credited with the actual investment return. Most of the early policies were invested in interest-paying instruments, but later the insurance companies offered equity-based investment policies.

Insurance companies now market their products through financial advisors and financial planners, as well as insurance agents. Insurance companies have developed a host of products with a variety of benefit plans. Many of their products, including universal life policies, benefit from investments made by the insurance company. The companies have become asset managers as much as insurance providers.

Derivative contracts were primarily developed by institutional trading houses. A financial advisor could not directly invest their clients' money in many of the new derivatives, which could only be traded on a large scale and took very specialized expertise to create. This was a major evolution in the securities industry. The financial advisor was no longer the cook who mixed and prepared a portfolio of stocks, but acted more like a waiter delivering products prepared in a large industrial kitchen.

Securities regulations passed in the 1930s fixed the minimum commissions brokers could charge. Brokerage firms could charge more but they could not charge less. The regulations were intended to ensure sufficient competition by protecting the brokerage firms from price competition that could bankrupt them. Initially, commission rates were based on a 100-share trade, and varied according to the stock price. The total commission on large trades, therefore, was multiples of the rate for the first 100 shares. There were no discounts for larger trades. By the late 1960s, fixed commissions were adjusted, and the cost per share decreased for larger transactions. Rates were the same for all firms, so there was still no price competition.

Many people advocated the elimination of fixed commissions, bringing free market competition to the securities industry. In May 1975, the rules were changed to allow negotiated commission rates. The deregulation of commissions became known in the securities industry as May Day. Many in the industry were alarmed by the changes, fearing the wholesale failure of inefficient firms no longer able to compete. Large trading firms tried to hold on to commission rates that were fairly close to the old regulated fixed rates, but institutional investors pushed them to cut commissions. Some institutions negotiated "unbundled commissions," which separated the costs for executing orders, providing research, and other services. Rates fell significantly, especially the costs for trading mutual funds and for the investment advisors who managed portfolios.

The new pricing competition brought about by the elimination of fixed commissions allowed new discount firms to enter the market offering low transaction rates for both individuals and institutions. One of the first discount brokerage firms was Charles Schwab. Others quickly followed. These were execution-only firms. Investors could open an account and place orders, but received no research or financial advice.

At first, the large wirehouse firms did not take the discounters seriously. They felt superior to the discounters and told clients and each other that the discounters would never seriously compete with the old white-shoe firms. In truth, the wirehouses and the discount firms executed smaller orders through the very same electronic Direct Order Transmission (DOT) system. For over-the-counter trades, the discounters frequently provided better-priced executions because they shopped for the best deals. Many of the wirehouses, on the other hand, directed all their over-the-counter orders to their own traders, who were suppose to match the best offer on the street, but didn't always adhere to that promise. As more firms entered the market, some competed with even lower fees, while others provided more services than discount brokerages and charged fees that were greater than the discount firms but still less than the big wirehouses.

The arrival of discount brokerage firms marked the beginning of the "self-help" era of securities investing. With more information available from sources other than financial advisors, the "do it yourself" bargain shoppers could stay reasonably informed. Discount firms' share of trading volume steadily increased until the wirehouses were forced to offer discounted commissions and increase the amount, variety, quality and volume of services they provided.

Historically, home mortgages were provided by savings and loan companies and banks that took in deposits and directly lent those deposits in the form of home mortgages. Each institution's ability to provide mortgages depended on their individual deposits. Banks in some parts of the country had more money to lend than they had a demand for. Other locations had more demand than they had deposits to lend. This changed when federal agencies began to buy mortgages from financial institutions. Lending institutions continued to originate and service mortgages. Securities firms also began to purchase mortgages and would then package them in trusts that were sold to investors, a process known as securitizing the mortgages.

These securities, known as Government National Mortgage Association (GNMA) mortgage pools and Collateral Mortgage Obligations (CMOs), could be traded like any other fixed-income security. Pension funds and individual investors increasingly bought these new low-risk securities. The savings and loan companies and banks that originated the mortgages made sure every mortgage they sold conformed to a standard set of rules, so buyers would be able to assign risk and secondary pricing to the investment.

Mortgage companies began to compete with the banks to originate and service mortgages, creating a whole new profession brokering mortgages to banks and mortgage companies. It was not long before securities firms were able to have their financial advisors paid for introducing their clients to mortgage companies. Financial advisors could in this way have a positive impact on both the assets and liabilities of their clients.

Brokerages and their mortgage subsidiaries created new products to provide the best lending terms for their investment clients, such as interest-only loans and no-down-payment loans that used securities to collateralize the required equity in the property. By holding the pledged securities in a brokerage account, clients could trade securities without moving them between accounts, and did not require any oversight by the firm except to ensure the account maintained sufficient equity to meet minimum requirements.

With the securitization of mortgages, investment bankers saw an opportunity to create additional products, including a new way to buy CMOs and slice them into pieces of principal payments and interest-only payments that matured at different times. An investor could own only the last principal payments, for example, realizing very high returns should there be an early loan payoff or early refinancing, but providing only minimal cash-flow payments and exposing them to the largest number of defaults.

Tax laws in the 1970s provided very generous tax benefits for accelerated depreciation on oil and gas exploration and commercial real estate. These tax incentives were so lucrative that the tax benefits alone made the investments profitable, almost regardless of the investment's performance. As a result, a new industry was created. Companies in the real estate or oil and gas industries worked with financial firms to create limited partnerships that benefited from the tax advantages.

Other industries soon formed similar partnerships, in railroad cars, shipping containers, cattle, nut and fruit groves, oil rigs, computer leasing, windmills and many other industries. Congress eventually closed the loopholes in the tax code and the IRS disallowed partnerships that were clearly abusive.

In the late 1970s, Merrill Lynch introduced the Cash Management Account (CMA). Fortune magazine said at the time that it was the most significant financial event of the latter half of the 20th century. The CMA integrated all of a client's financial accounts, consolidating their short and long-term investing, check writing, savings, debit accounts and margin borrowing into a single account. The CMA automatically accessed money for checking and credit cards, and moved funds among securities accounts, money funds and margin accounts.

Because the Glass-Steagall Act still separated investment and commercial banking, Merrill Lynch worked with Bank One, located in Columbus, Ohio, to provide banking services for check writing and credit card processing, electronically linked to the primary Merrill Lynch account. The CMA initially met with resistance from Merrill Lynch's brokers and their clients, but was relentlessly championed by the company's CEO, Donald Regan. His insistence that the firm offer CMAs probably made a greater contribution to Merrill Lynch's success than anything else he did during his tenure.

Soon after Merrill Lynch introduced the CMA, all the other major firms did so as well. The success of the CMAs was aided by the introduction of the Automatic Teller Machine (ATM). Merrill Lynch managed large amounts of money, but did not handle cash. Banks were very reluctant to cash checks drawn on checking accounts at other banks, particularly if the banks were in another state. Bank One was only located in Ohio. ATMs provided access to cash for CMA customers.

The first prototype ATM machine was introduced in 1969. Today, they dispense $670 billion in cash every year in the United States alone. Many banking executives claim ATMs kept them from going out of business. Another breakthrough occurred when ATMs began to accept Visa, MasterCard and other credit cards. By using credit card processing systems, each bank did not have to maintain their own unique ATM processing systems. Today, credit cards dispense local currency around the world at current exchange rates free of dealer mark-ups.

A Period of Growth: The 1980s

Many industries and professions benefited from the strong economy and bull markets of the 1980s, while others struggled with the new climate of deregulation, competition, globalization, greater consumer access to information, and the continuing transition of the American economy from manufacturing to service industries.

President Reagan's policies helped improve the economy as it emerged from the recession of the late 1970s. Reagan expanded and accelerated government mandated deregulation begun under the Carter administration, which helped make many industries more competitive. Reagan's tax policies put more money into the hands of consumers. Reagan's plans to decrease the size of government through spending cuts, however, were never fully implemented. Massive Defense Department budgets were approved to pursue the ongoing Cold War arms race with the Soviet Union. Without the necessary spending cuts, Reagan's tax cuts resulted in record federal deficits.

Deregulation dramatically changed many industries, including telecommunications and the airline industry. Proponents of deregulation felt consumers were being hurt by a lack of competition, and targeted large companies they considered monopolies. The most obvious example was American Telegraph and Telephone (AT&T), which controlled over 80 percent of local phone service throughout the country and most of the long distance service. Nine new companies emerged from the breakup of AT&T. Local service was split among seven new regional "baby bells." Lucent was created to handle research and technology. AT&T remained to provide only long distance service. While the baby bells had an advantage in local service, competition was encouraged in the long distance market and for all other phone services.

The economy improved considerably in the 1980s. The decade began with one of the largest and longest periods of investment gains in market history. The stock market soared from a DOW of 1,000 in 1980 to a peak of 2,663 just before it crashed on October 11, 1987. The markets were helped by the passage in 1981 of the Economic Recovery Act, which established "universal" IRAs for all workers. The growing number of defined contribution retirement accounts increased assets available for investing in securities. Interest rates declined through the 1980s, providing relief from the high rates of the late 1970s and early 1980s. Lower interest rates further contributed to the burgeoning economy of the

1980s. The U.S. economy was also bolstered by declining oil prices. The Organization of Petroleum Exporting Countries (OPEC) failed to control oil production among its members, precipitating a steep decline in oil prices and an eventual price collapse in 1986.

On October 11, 1987, the market bubble finally burst. The DOW dropped 500 points, losing 25 percent of its value over two days. Investors' increasingly leveraged positions, achieved through the use of derivatives and encouraged by financial experts and institutions, exacerbated losses. Investors reacted very differently to the 1987 crash, however, than they did to previous market crashes. Instead of selling their holdings after the big market drop, they bought more stocks at the suddenly reduced prices, helping the market recover. Although the crash caused a great deal of damage, a sustained recovery began shortly afterwards, and the markets ended with a three percent net gain for the year.

As the economy recovered from the disruptions of the 1970s, retail sales and distribution increased. Specialty stores were introduced that focused on a single brand, such as Gap, Nike and Banana Republic. Some specialty stores sold only a single brand of products for a specific age group, such as Gap, Gap Kids and Baby Gap. Specialty products were developed for narrowly defined niche markets. The food industry, for example, could no longer cater to "average American" tastes. Salad bars, organic food stores, nutritional supplement stores, sushi bars, juice bars and countless other niche market restaurants opened in the 1980s.

Service sector employers put a greater value on education than those in the manufacturing sector, so the shift from a manufacturing to a service sector economy helped Americans who had more education, and hurt those who had less. In 1967, the median annual income of a person with one to three years of high school education was 95 percent of the median income for all people in the workforce. By 1974, it was 83 percent. In 1980, a high school dropout earned only 72 percent of the median national income. By 1990, it had dropped to 59 percent. The median income of those who have completed high school, compared to the median incomes of all workers, has declined from 113 percent in 1967 to 93 percent in 1990. The median income of high school graduates, compared to those who completed four years of college, has declined from 70 percent in 1967 to 57 percent in 1990. Undoubtedly, these divergent trends have continued and the situation is even more extreme today.

Increasing access to information drove many economic and social changes in the 1980s. The rise of personal computers in the 1980s enabled consumers to better collect, organize and disseminate information. Many large consumer product companies that dominated their markets early in the century struggled to survive in the new environment.

The same was true for some large financial companies, as central asset accounts sucked billions of dollars out of bank checking and saving accounts in the 1980s. Historically high short-term interest rates benefited the holders of Central Asset Accounts. Money market funds, including those associated with Central Asset Accounts, were paying 15 to 18 percent interest rates. Banks were paying less than half that. Central asset accounts gave customers better access to their cash while providing extraordinarily high money market returns. As deposits flowed into money market accounts, less money was available for banks to lend, which reduced their profits. In order to compete with central asset accounts, banks were forced to pay increasingly higher interest rates on money market accounts and to offer integrated checking and savings vehicles.

Options also grew in popularity during the 1980s. In 1983, the CBOE introduced trading on options based on broad indexes, such as the Russell 100 and S&P 500 indexes. By 1984, the option market's annual volume exceeded 100 million contracts. In 1989, the CBOE began trading interest rate option products.

Financial planning as a professional service was quite rare in the early 1970s. Most financial planning was conducted by accountants and CPAs, and only when their clients requested it. Estate planning had historically been the domain of insurance specialists and attorneys, who worked to minimize estate taxes at death, rather than maximize retirement income. In the mid-1970s, the Stanford Research Institute published a report on financial services that recognized a need for more financial planning services. People were living longer and needed to plan for potentially decades of retirement. Due to the ballooning cost of college tuition, they also needed financial planning to provide for the education of their children.

Nevertheless, the growing need for financial planning did not become broadly recognized until the early 1980s, when the opportunity to provide more services to clients, increase fee income, and build a stronger client relationship enticed many professionals to offer financial planning. Estate attorneys, CPAs, insurance agents and financial advisors all began to provide planning services. A number of computer programs were also introduced; clients could fill out a questionnaire and the program produced a financial plan. One of the first firms created specifically to provide financial planning was Kendrick and Stimpfig. Drexel Burnham later purchased Kendrick and Stimpfig to become the first brokerage firm to provide financial planning.

There was little professional training, few standardized formats, and no professional designations or accreditations for financial planners until the Certified Financial Planner Board of Standards was founded in 1985. The Certified Financial Planner Board of Standards established practices and standards for professional financial planners, and provided professional education programs and certification testing. The Certified Financial Planner (CFP) accreditation was created in 1985. Many universities and other educational organizations began to provide training, preparation and testing for the CFP certification. Over 36,000 people now hold the CFP designation.

A New Economy: The 1990s

The 1990s was a period of transformation for the American economy. The decline of American manufacturing was balanced by the meteoric ascent of the technology sector. The securities markets saw their largest percentage gains in securities prices of the century in the 1990s, but the economic and social changes wrought by growing foreign competition led to troubling increases in education and income disparity.

The Berlin Wall was dismantled November 9, 1989.

The Soviet Union collapsed on December 17, 1991, separating into 13 new countries. America was recognized as the world's single "superpower." The United States demonstrated its strength when Iraq invaded Kuwait in August 1990. Leading a broad allied coalition that included several Arab countries, the United States initiated attacks on January 17, 1991. The Gulf War was over by March 3, 1991. In six weeks, the United States had removed Iraqi forces from Kuwait, crippled Iraqi military capabilities, and established no-fly zones in Northern and Southern Iraq.

After 12 years of Republican administrations, the country elected a two-term democratic president, William Jefferson Clinton, in 1992. The 1990s saw the rise of an increasingly polarized electorate, and a caustically-partisan domestic political environment that led to a failed impeachment attempt in 1999.

The federal debt was addressed by tax increases implemented by both the George H.W. Bush and Clinton administrations. Aided by a soaring economy, the lowest unemployment in decades, and welfare reforms that decreased expenditures, the federal government created the largest budget surpluses in U.S. history.

The DOW average escalated from 2,700 to 11,497 in the 1990s. Interest rates fell to 50-year lows. Many investors saw the value of their portfolios quadruple. The technology revolution, fueled by venture capital and the IPO market, created a vast array of new companies and new investment opportunities. What Federal Reserve Chief Alan Greenspan at the time referred to as the stock market's "excess exuberance," however, led to a market bubble in the 1990s that finally burst at the turn of the century.

Not everyone benefited from the market's precipitous climb in the 1990s. Using constant dollars from 1967 to 1990, the median income for all workers increased from $32,939 to $40,393 during the decade. The mean income, though, increased from $37,489 to $50,266. The difference between the median and the mean income decreased from 88 percent to 80 percent, revealing a significant proportionate shift in income to the country's top earners.

New companies were created and old companies were transformed in the 1990s by advancements in information and communication technologies, particularly the advent of the Internet. Increases in the processing power of personal computers, coupled with new software and the Internet's communication abilities were used to advertise, purchase, deliver and implement products and services at dramatically lower cost.

Satellite and fiber optic transmission, mobile phones, e-mail, electronic document transmission and other communication technology developments and improvements facilitated increasing foreign competition and the rise of a global economy, which had a major impact on the United States. Increasing global competition and the desire to limit labor costs encouraged companies to outsource the production of goods, furthering America's transition to a service sector economy. American companies purchased components from all over the world in the 1990s, and manufactured finished products wherever the cheapest labor was located. The American economy had been supported for centuries by its agricultural sector, which is now a very small part of the economy and even smaller part of the workforce.

Even work done by the service sector, once thought immune to foreign competition, was increasingly being outsourced overseas.

International trade was further aided by new and amended trade agreements. The process of negotiating individual agreements for each product and country was recognized in the 1980s as a serious impediment to international commerce. Discussions that led to the Uruguay round of negotiations to amend the 1947 General Agreement on Tariffs and Trade began as early as 1982 and continued until 1993. The new agreements were finally signed by ministers from most of the 125 participating governments on April 15, 1994.

The United States, Mexico and Canada adopted the North American Free Trade Agreement (NAFTA) in 1994 to help eliminate trade and investment barriers. The World Trade Organization (WTO) was established in 1995 to help determine standards of trade and judge trade rule infractions.

The European Union (EU), originally known as the European Community (EC) or European Economic Community (EEC), was created in November of 1993 to help establish common policies and trade agreements among its now 25 European members, a majority of which also share a common currency. In the 1990s, the securities industry benefited from the strong economy, growth in the financial markets and an increase in retirement investment opportunities. In current dollars, the industry's value doubled during the decade. In adjusted dollars, the sector grew by 50 percent. As a percentage of the economy, it increased from 17.4 percent of the GDP to 20.6 percent. Commercial banking grew at a seven percent rate compared to almost no growth for saving banks, many of which were bought by commercial banks. Credit unions grew a bit faster than commercial banks, about eight percent annually. Asset-backed securities increased by 20 percent annually, until almost every type of debt, from credit card debt to car loans, were securitized and sold on the secondary market as fixed income investments. The continuing shift to defined contribution plans in the 1990s led to further growth in the mutual fund industry. Most defined contribution plans offered mutual funds as their primary investment vehicles. By 1995, mutual fund assets topped $1 trillion.

Derivatives also continued to grow in popularity. In 1990, the CBOE introduced long-term options called LEAPS. Option trading on the DOW average began in 1997. By 1998, annual trading volume had grown to 200 million contracts. By 2000, it had grown to 300 million.

In 1993, Exchange Traded Funds (ETFs) were introduced. ETFs are derivative products traded on the listed exchanges that mimic specific market indexes, sectors, or specific industries. ETFs provide distinct advantages for investors, speculators and asset managers. If an investor feels individual stocks within a particular industry or sector are too risky, while they believe the industry as a whole is promising, they can use an ETF to invest in the entire industry or sector. ETFs do not incur management costs, so investors can inexpensively focus on particular market sectors. The S&P 500 ETF, for example, allows traders, market timers or managers to easily hedge the risk in a portfolio. ETFs have been one of the fastest growing financial product lines in recent years. By 1998, about $10 billion in assets were invested in ETFs.

ETFs can also confuse investors, however, who may not fully understand their leveraging and hedging elements. ETFs are many steps removed from the simple stock-picking strategies once taught by Benjamin Graham, known as the father of value investing, or traditional equity sector portfolio allocation. The number and complexity of investment products is one of the reasons investors increasingly seek the help of financial advisors.

The risk of derivatives, and the fallibility of the vaunted financial professionals and advisors who promoted them, was clear when Long Term Capital, a historically-successful investment firm that used a lot of leverage and a great number of derivatives, collapsed in 1998. The Federal Reserve and some major Wall Street firms stepped in to prevent a major collapse of the markets. They successfully stabilized the markets, but from then on, everyone knew that even a firm with some of the most successful managers in the industry could leverage its investments to such an extent through the use of derivatives that it could bring the whole system tumbling down.

Opportunities to invest in the markets through retirement plans continued to increase in the 1990s. In 1996, the Small Business Job Protection Act allowed for tax-favored SIMPLE (Savings Incentive Match Plan for Employees) retirement plans for small business employees. A year later, the Taxpayer Relief Act of 1997 created IRAs and Roth IRAs for after-tax contributions that incurred no taxes (on the funds or their earnings) upon withdrawal. The Taxpayer Relief Act also eliminated portfolio management restrictions that disadvantaged fund shareholders. Insurance and government financial services had the slowest growth in the financial sector. Life insurance grew at just over half the rate of commercial banks and credit unions. As the Federal National Mortgage Association and similar agencies began to perform more of the government's traditional roles, they grew much faster than the government sector, becoming a very significant part of the economy. Private pension funds, for example, grew almost twice as quickly as government retirement funds.

Noticeable increases in consumer access to information that began in the 1980s accelerated in the 1990s with the development of the Internet. For some financial services clients, the complexity, variety and quantity of information available was confusing and overwhelming. Educating and guiding clients became one of the most valuable services provided by financial professionals.

New business and marketing concepts emerged in the 1990s. "Guerilla marketing" and "viral marketing" were developed to attract consumer attention, or in the parlance of the time, "capture mindshare." Some companies focused on Internet traffic and "mindshare" to the exclusion of revenues. Some Internet companies seemed more concerned with measuring the number of "hits" on their Web site than they were with turning a profit. Many people championed a new business paradigm that relied on unfounded speculation and unsupported valuations. "New economy" analysts based their forecasts on Internet traffic and potential revenue growth. Traditional valuations that focused on earnings were considered relics of the "old economy." Some companies that had limited or nonexistent revenues and enormous losses traded at share prices that gave them market capitalizations of several billion dollars. The tech bubble was well on its way to exploding by the end of the decade.

A New Reality: 2000 and Beyond

The new century began with one of the closest elections in history. George W. Bush won the Electoral College count, though he lost the popular vote count. On September 11, 2001, terrorists attacked the United States by flying commercial airplanes into the New York World Trade Center towers and the Pentagon. A fourth plane likely headed for Washington, D.C. was grounded in Pennsylvania by passengers who overtook the terrorists before they could reach their target. Around 3,000 people died in the attacks.

The Bush administration and Congress passed the largest tax cuts ever. A number of tax preferences used by wealthy people and some corporations were eliminated, but the tax code overall become more complex than ever. Promised spending cuts never materialized. In 2003, the United States launched a preemptive war on Iraq. The cost of the war and the rebuilding of Iraq, the continuing price of rebuilding Afghanistan, decreasing tax revenues, spending for homeland security, and enumerable pork barrel projects pushed the federal budget from its largest surpluses to its greatest deficits in American history.

The new century also witnessed massive corporate fraud by American businesses, and significant securities abuses by investment bankers and securities analysts. Some companies falsified financial statements to inflate stock earnings and covered up outright theft of company assets by executives. Some energy companies manipulated the newly deregulated free-market trading of electric power to drive prices up to as much as 100 times their previous rates. Some states were unable to purchase enough power to meet their needs, causing temporary blackouts.

In response to these abuses, Congress passed the Sarbanes-Oxley Act of 2002, which placed much higher standards for corporate accounting and reporting, and required corporate CEOs to be personally accountable for the accuracy of their company's financial reports. The fraud committed by corporate executives, investment bankers and research analysts spawned numerous penal and civil lawsuits. Investment bankers and securities analysts faced civil suits, criminal charges and regulatory punishment. Several highly-paid corporate executives received long jail terms for their convictions.

Globalization and mechanization in the new century hastened the transition to a service-sector economy. About one-third of the entire population lived and worked on farms at the beginning of the twentieth century. By the 2000 census, the percentage of the workforce employed in agriculture had dropped to seven tenths of one percent. International competition and the introduction of new, highly productive technologies, including robotic assembly machines, decreased manufacturing sector employment in the early 20th century. Goods that required human hands to produce, such as clothing, appliances or circuitry, were imported from less developed nations where wages, benefits and working facilities cost a fraction of those in the United Sates. Around two-thirds of everything sold in Wal-Mart, a company whose early motto was "made in America," is now manufactured overseas.

Employment growth in the last 20 years has been almost exclusively in areas requiring an educated workforce. Service occupations grew from 13.9 million in 1983 to 19.2 million by 2002, a 44 percent increase. Managerial and professional specialty jobs increased 80 percent, from 23.6 million to 42.5 million. Technical, sales and administrative support grew only 24 percent, from 31.3 million to 38.9 million jobs. In 1967, the average income of Americans with one to three years of high school, measured in constant 2001 dollars, was $31,255, which was equal to 95 percent of the median income for all workers.

While employment growth has been in areas requiring an educated workforce, the educational advantage once held by the United States has considerably eroded. While educational standards in other countries have improved, America's have deteriorated. Along with advancements in communications technologies, the shift in educational assets has increased service sector outsourcing. Clerical, technical, and even professional service work can now be quickly conveyed to educated, lower-paid employees in other countries, most notably in India and China. Outsourcing has grown exponentially in the last five years, and now includes everything from computer programming to telemarketing to X-ray processing.

Suburbanization shaped the American landscape, housing economy, and society in the last 30 years. Many major cities in the country became "donut" cities

— poorer urban areas encircled by affluent suburban neighborhoods. "White flight" sapped cities of wealth, jobs and culture, resulting in a more segregated society. Many highways were initially built so people living in the new suburbs would have better transportation to their jobs in the cities. Jobs also moved to the suburbs, however, so some people living in cities now commute to work in the suburbs.

The markets were soaring at the beginning of the century. From 1992 to 2002, financial assets in the United States increased by 250 percent, representing an eight percent compound rate of growth, which was much greater than the rate for the economy as a whole, only about three percent. The number of investors also increased dramatically in the last 20 years. By 1983, 42.4 million people representing 15.9 million households owned equities. By 2002, 84.2 million individuals and 52.7 households owned equities. In March 2000, technology stocks pushed the NASDAQ exchange to a record high of 5,047.69. In the ensuing crash, many new companies went bankrupt, billions of dollars were lost in declining securities markets, and many people saw their pensions and 401(k) retirement plans lose much or all of their value.

By 2004, the economy had largely recovered from the market collapse, September 11th and the invasion of Iraq. The securities markets also recovered to begin another phase of growth. Market increases were in part encouraged by the passage of the Economic Growth and Tax Relief Reconciliation Act in 2001, which expanded retirement savings opportunities for American workers. By 2001, the combined finance and insurance industries had grown to 452,000 businesses with 6.248 million employees representing an annual payroll of $373.6 billion. Within just the securities sector of the market, there were 76,900 businesses by 2001, with 947,100 employees representing an annual payroll of $125 billion. There were 172,100 investment bankers and traders, 381,100 securities brokers, 171,500 portfolio management firms and 83,400 investment advisors.

From 1985 to 2003, the value of publicly-traded financial sector stocks, as measured by the Standard and Poor's 500 Index, grew from 8.1 percent of the S&P index to 17.8 percent. The only sector of the economy that has grown faster than the financial sector in the last 20 years is health care. Most of this growth occurred from 1970 to the late 1990s. In the past five years, however, the number of firms has stagnated. The number of financial advisors peaked in 2001 and has fallen since.

Discounting in the securities industry increased in the early 21st century, facilitated by advancements in software and communications. Virtual securities firms were created on the Internet providing online information and trade executions with no physical brick and mortar locations, no financial planning services, and only as many registered representatives as were required to satisfy NASD regulations. Some offered trades for as little as $7 each. The Internet firms enabled clients to access their investment accounts and use many other features, such as online bill paying and transferring money between accounts, without ever speaking to a financial advisor. In some cases, the only people a client could speak to directly were those providing Internet site technical support.

At first, major brokerage firms ignored the new Internet upstarts the same way they had ignored discount firms in the 1970s. Eventually, even traditional wirehouses like Morgan Stanley began to provide online trading, though not as highly discounted as the online and discount firms. Merrill Lynch originally resisted online trading, considering it a form of "gambling," but eventually Merrill Lynch offered online trading, though more tightly controlled to help keep clients from overextending themselves.

In order to compete with the new Internet firms and the online wirehouse firms, traditional discounters like Charles Schwab began to offer even deeper discounted online trading, as well as some financial advice and other services, focusing on a niche between the inexpensive online firms that provided few or no services, and the more expensive full-service wirehouse companies.

Schwab's strategy proved effective at first, as many of the "do it yourself" investors who lost their money in the technology crash migrated back to firms with greater resources and more services. Internet investors who had pursued quick profits prior to the crash, investing in the most volatile and risky stocks, lost the most in its aftermath. All brokerage firms suffered a decline in business, but the Internet firms were hardest hit. Many Internet companies went out of business or merged with larger firms. Some analysts declared the "self-help" era was over. The firms that survived, like E-trade and Ameritrade, began offering other products, such as banking and mortgage services. The Internet will probably continue to be used as a cost-efficient platform for trading, but will likely never serve as a substitute for professional financial advisors.

Advancements in media and communications have dramatically increased investors' access to information and financial advice. Current market information and analyst research reports were only available 40 years ago by calling a broker during market hours. In most areas of the country, there were only a few television stations, which devoted less than five minutes to the stock market in their daily news programs. Local newspapers outside large metropolitan markets published a limited list of stock quotes that reflected the opening prices of the previous market day. Subscribers to the Wall Street Journal outside large metropolitan areas received their editions a day late. A summary of information and statistics was available in Barron's newspaper, which was published weekly. Business Week magazine was also a weekly, but was only available by subscription to people who could prove they were corporate officers. Fortune and Forbes magazines were the leading business magazines, but were only published monthly. Other than these limited and out-of-date sources, brokers controlled all the investment information. Financial news publishing has greatly expanded in recent years, filling magazine racks and bookstores with business, finance and investing information.

In the 1980s, major networks and cable stations recognized the need for financial information and began to offer extended market programs, such as "Lou Rukeyser's Wall Street" on CNBC and Lou Dobbs' program on PBS. As the number of cable networks increased, some were introduced that exclusively provide financial market news, such as MSNBC and FNN. Financial news stations can now be seen in offices, sports bars, restaurants and airports. These stations, however, package financial news and showcase experts in a fashion that is entertaining, but frequently lacks substantive information required by investors.

The Internet has developed into a major conduit for financial news. Hundreds of sites provide market and investment information. Many of the new sights are free to users, relying solely on advertising for revenue, while others charge modest fees. Few sites offer useful advice, however. Most provide only market information, or revise what other firms and publications have reported. Many companies now frequently announce earnings and company information on their Web sites. Individual investors can watch the same announcements at the same time as the business journalists, but do not receive much objective analysis from the companies.

Today, we have an information glut. The stock market has become a national spectator sport. Financial information was once provided only by brokers, filtered to address an individual client's issues or interests, now be obtained virtually anytime, anyplace.

Advancements in information and communications technologies impacted the securities industry in other ways as well. Forty years ago, most brokerage firms had not adopted electronic quote machines; they were still using teletype communication for information and order transmission. Today, trades are instantly conveyed by electronic means.

In the 1950s, banks, insurance companies and brokerage firms exclusively dealt their own products using their own sales forces. Today, it is sometimes difficult to tell them apart. Financial companies are scrambling to form new alliances to provide a greater diversity of products and services to their customers. Brokerage firms are lending money and collecting short-term deposits in money market accounts, banks are selling insurance and securities, insurance companies loan money and base many of their products on equity investments, and tax accountants are selling securities products.

Mergers, subsidiaries and contractual agreements have frayed the legal lines separating banks, investment banks, securities brokerages and insurance companies. In April 1998, Travelers, an insurance company that owned the investment house Salomon Smith Barney, announced a merger with Citicorp, the parent of Citibank, to create the world's largest financial services company. The merger was approved on a temporary ruling by banking regulators. Faced with an obvious infringement of the Glass-Steagall Act of 1933, intended to separate commercial and investment functions, but pressured by an intense lobbying effort by Citicorp and Travelers, a deeply divided House of Representatives passed legislation by one vote in May 1998 that allows for the merging of banks, securities firms, and insurance companies. In 1999, after 12 attempts in 25 years, Congress repealed the Glass-Steagall Act. Other institutions took advantage of the rule changes, moving to create mergers like Citicorp-Travelers.

Tax law changes made in 2001 introduced a college savings plan commonly called a "529 plan" (named after its section in the Internal Revenue code). Health savings accounts, introduced in January 2004, allowed individuals and families to set aside money tax-free for medical expenses. The new 529 college savings plans and health savings accounts created more vehicles for purchasing mutual funds.

Mutual fund assets in the United States grew from $448 million in 296,000 accounts in 1940 to $7.4 trillion in 261 million accounts by the end of 2003. These were split between money market funds with $2.052 trillion in assets, equity funds with $3.685 trillion, bond funds with $1.241 trillion, and hybrid funds with assets of $437 billion.

From two mutual funds in 1924, the number increased to 100 by the end of 1929, and 1,243 by the end of 1984. Since 1940, the mutual fund classification has expanded to include "open-ended" funds, "closed-end" funds, unit investment trusts and "exchange-traded" funds, though some of these forms are rarely used today. Tri-Continental and Lehman funds, for example, are two of the early U.S. closed-end funds still trading today.

By the end of 2003, there were 8,100 separate funds, including 4,601 equity funds, of which 2,933 were capital appreciation funds, 509 hybrid funds, 2,043 bond funds and 973 money market funds. Within each of these categories, there were funds of every variety and purpose: core, growth, value, large cap, mid cap, small cap, micro cap, single-country funds, single-industry funds, socially-conscious funds, concentrated funds, index funds and many others. The list of available mutual funds continues to expand every year.

Eighty percent of households that own mutual funds participated in employer-sponsored defined contribution retirement plans. Retirement plans represent 48 percent of household fund purchases. Thirty-seven percent of mutual funds are purchased by individuals through financial advisors. Ten percent are purchased directly from mutual fund companies. Only five percent of sales occur through discount brokers.

Seventy-seven percent of mutual funds are purchased by individuals, either directly or through retirement plans. Taxable household accounts represent 33 percent of mutual fund assets. Forty-four percent are tax-deferred household accounts in IRAs, 401(k)s and other retirement plans. Only eight percent are tax-exempt funds and 15 percent are taxable non-household accounts. As of 2002, 51.5 percent of investors only own mutual funds, 11 percent only own individual stocks and 37.5 percent own both.

Households that own mutual funds have a median income of $68,000 and have median household financial assets of $125,000. People who make the mutual fund purchasing decisions for the household have a median age of 48 years. Seventy-one percent are married or living with a partner, 57 percent have college or post-graduate degrees and 77 percent are employed.

Independent investment advisors such as Fidelity and the Capital Group were used as intermediaries by 60 percent of financial advisors. Banks and thrifts were used by 20 percent, insurance companies by 14 percent, and brokerage wirehouse firms by six percent.

There are hundreds of mutual fund complexes, but assets are distributed unevenly. Thirty-six percent of all assets are represented by the top five complexes, 48 percent by the top 10 and 72 percent by the top 25 complexes.

Mutual fund complexes have created an increasing number of specialty funds, mostly designed to target specific industries or other unique investment niches, or to mimic market indexes. In the late 1990s, equity mutual funds were introduced that focused on companies with similar capitalization sizes or investment styles. New categories were introduced based on the size of the company (large cap, mid cap, small cap) and the type of investment (value, growth, blend). A "style box" matrix using these new categories was developed to describe mutual fund investing. The idea was that the purchaser or advisor would be capable of knowing which style would perform best at any one time, and could manage risk using style allocations. There are few if any investment professionals, however, who have been consistently successful using style allocations to increase total portfolio returns.

The diversity and complexity of available mutual fund investments have created a greater need for financial advisors. Few people have access to all of the information they need to make educated fund purchases and ably monitor their investments. For example, the number of index funds is rapidly multiplying; investors require the guidance of a good financial advisor to pick the right index fund and the correct percentage of their portfolios that should be devoted to index funds. Investors need to be aware of changes occurring not only in the markets, but also in the mutual fund companies themselves. Mutual fund management companies can change ownership, employees, policies and investment strategies. Most investors cannot devote the time necessary to track all the changes in securities and the securities industry; they require professional advisors to stay informed.

The popularity and diversity of derivative products continues to increase in the early 21st century. Option contracts with different strike prices and expiration dates were produced for hundreds of different companies and indexes. In 2003, a record 640.2 million contracts were traded on the Chicago Mercantile Exchange. The CME now moves about $1.6 billion per day in settlement payments. By 2001, the market in Exchange Traded Funds (ETFs) had grown 10- fold since its inception, to over $100 billion. By June 2004, it had grown to just under $250 billion in assets. By 2003, the number of put and call contracts were so numerous that even the Wall Street Journal listed only a selection of contracts. You can now hedge the risk of climate irregularities, floods and earthquakes using OTC futures contracts. In 2003, the Chicago Climate Exchange was introduced, where companies can trade contracts on greenhouse gases as a free-market incentive for environmental management.

Hedge funds have become one of the most popular varieties of new investment products. Hedge funds can be extremely risky. Brokerage firms have diminished this risk by creating an additional type of trust called a "fund of funds" that purchases parts of several hedge funds. This does diversify the risk, but it also incurs another layer of fees for buyers, on top of hedge fund manager fees and profit sharing. There is currently a movement to establish regulatory and disclosure requirements for hedge funds similar to required mutual funds disclosures.

There has been astronomical growth in the number of hedge funds and the amount of money invested in them. Each hedge fund is restricted by law to qualified investors. The minimum hedge-fund investment is typically $1 million, and most purchasers are therefore usually wealthier individuals. People who invest money in hedge funds often do not know exactly what the fund actually owns, and may only know what the price of the fund is from periodic reporting. Most hedge fund managers receive an annual management fee of two percent and also receive a percentage of the net profits, usually about 20 percent. When fund of funds for hedge funds are created to provide diversification, the fund of funds manager gets an additional annual management fee of one percent and 10 percent of the remaining profits after the individual fund managers get paid both their management and percentage fee. That is a lot of management fees to be paid out of investors' profits.

Hedge funds are currently not regulated and are allowed to use aggressive strategies unavailable to mutual funds, including short selling, leveraging, program trading, swaps, arbitrage and derivatives. One common approach is the long/short strategy. A hedge fund manager will own stocks they think will outperform the market and short the stocks they think will underperform the market. If the market goes up, they are betting the stocks they own, called long positions, will go up more than the stocks they are shorting. If the market goes down, they are betting their short positions will go down more than their long positions. Sometimes managers will own or short stocks and then offset their positions with derivatives. Some try to take advantage of the spread between interest rates in different maturities of bonds, or between junk bonds, corporate bonds and government bonds.

The basic strategy behind hedge funds is to take advantage of inefficiencies in the market. The increase in the number of players looking for inefficiencies, however, has greatly decreased the inefficiencies. The inefficiencies margins have gotten smaller and the number of attractive opportunities has decreased. Hedge fund managers have responded by developing new, bolder strategies. Some very large funds have even begun buying and selling entire private companies.

Some people are losing their affection for hedge funds. There is a concern there is too much money chasing market inefficiencies and the historic returns hedge funds have enjoyed will no longer be possible. There is also the concern that too many new hedge funds are being created, and there may not be enough talented managers to successfully manage them. Some fear the same problems that arose from the proliferation of venture funds in the 1990s, too much money chasing too few opportunities with too much pressure to invest, may also plague hedge funds in the future.

Historically, institutions and large private investors hired professional investment advisors to manage their assets on a discretionary basis. They frequently used more than one manger, employing the managers' varying talents to increase the success and diversification of their investments. Accounts were usually held to a minimum of $1 million or more, as the cost of managing each account, which includes preparing reports and meeting with clients, was prohibitively high for smaller accounts. These minimum investment requirements prevented clients with smaller accounts from using individual portfolio managers.

Investors with smaller portfolios have used mutual funds to access professional management to increase the diversification and success of their investments, but mutual funds are not always optimal products for individual investors. Mutual funds are not tailored to individual needs. They are guided by a group of investors' general objectives. Unique individual circumstances, such as personal tax considerations, are not taken into account. An individual investor cannot influence the decisions of the fund manager, who can be changed with only limited notification, which can have a significant and unexpected impact on the fund's performance. In addition, a mutual fund is an existing portfolio, and can frequently contain capital gains liabilities or loses the new buyer acquires.

Investors and brokerage firms have long sought to find a way to economically provide individual professional account management. E.F. Hutton's James Lockwood is credited with creating the first platform in 1975 that could provide individual management for accounts as low as $100,000, which led to the Separately Managed Account (SMA) industry. SMAs use fee-based pricing for investment management services. All major firms now provide this service and there are many similar platforms available at smaller firms. Since 1996, assets managed by the SMA industry have grown 30 percent to 40 percent annually, reaching $795.2 billion in 2002.

The SMA platform enables investment managers to economically manage smaller accounts. The investment advisor will typically divide types of investors into "model portfolios" so they can manage several accounts at the same time. Investment advisors put instructions for the model portfolio into a system that sends execution orders for each account. SMA accounts usually have different securities depending on the attractiveness of individual stocks at the time the portfolio was created. However, because it is more efficient and provides consistent performance to all their clients, investment advisors usually manage their different accounts in a fairly similar way, so eventually most of the portfolios look very much the same.

In this model, there is seldom any direct contact between the client and the investment advisor. Communication with clients is performed by a "relationship manager" who works for the investment advisor's firm. The relationship manager frequently does not have the discretion to switch investment advisors who manage the portfolios. Financial advisors also work with investment advisors to provide SMAs, but using a financial advisor has distinct advantages. Unlike the relationship manager, The financial advisor can easily change portfolio managers if they are underperforming. The financial advisor can also better know their clients, determine their specific needs, and advocate for their particular goals than the relationship manager. Investors should be aware, though, that firms that employ financial advisors vary widely and apply different criteria to their selection of managers. Firms typically classify their managers by a specific risk category. The firm will usually assess the client's risk profile to determine which of its managers will work with the client.

The agreement that binds the client, investment manager, and brokerage firm contains a single fee paid by the client that includes the financial advisor's compensation, the investment manager's fee, all commissions on transactions, and the cost of quarterly reports that include comparative performance analyses. SMA accounts , also called "wrap accounts" because all the services and costs are wrapped into one account with a single fee. Wrap accounts provide a much more individualized product for clients, and have an intermediary financial advisor to help clients monitor account performance. They are one of the fastest-growing types of investment products now offered in the securities industry.

Initially, the standard annual fee for a wrap account was three percent of total assets, similar to the total fees and costs a client incurs for a mutual fund. Mutual fund fees range from 10 to 15 basis points for index funds to a range of just under one percent to 2.5 percent for actively-managed accounts. What is not included in annual mutual fund fees is the compensation paid to the brokerage firm and the commission costs on transactions. Competition and client pressure has driven down the three percent wrap fee, which is vulnerable because it is fully disclosed. Clients tend to object to fees when they are fully disclosed. The brokerage commissions paid by mutual funds are not disclosed and not part of the annual fees that are disclosed by mutual funds. A sliding scale is now usually employed. The fee decreases as the size of the account increases. Most firms apply fees to the total of all SMA accounts held by the client. If a client has more than one account with the firm, the value of all the accounts combined is used to set the fee, even if the client uses different managers. In general, fees have dropped to between 1.5 percent and 2.5 percent.

During many periods, many mutual funds and investment advisors have not performed as well as their market benchmarks. Investors lamented that there was no easy way for them to receive an average market return, which was usually better than they could get picking stocks themselves or having their broker or investment advisor do it. It was not feasible for an individual investor to buy the quantities of stocks in the proportions necessary to match the index performance. Vanguard and John Boggle helped introduce a type of mutual fund that matched the S&P index. Because the portfolio was relatively static, with little turnover, management fees were very low, so the funds did come very close to matching the performance of the index. Index funds proved to be very popular. Competing index funds were introduced and other funds were created to match other indexes. In some cases, managers used indexes based on derivatives, options and futures.

Index funds can wisely be used as the core investment in a broader investment strategy. It can be difficult to overcome management fees and transaction costs and still consistently beat the market as measured by a specific index. An increasingly common strategy is to put a significant part of an equity portfolio in a core managed account or a broad market index fund, such as the S&P 500, and then to use specialty managers in specific areas, such as emerging markets, country specific foreign funds, industry specific funds, indexed funds, hedge funds or other higher-risk investments to boost returns while increasing diversification.

The modern securities industry would be unrecognizable to those who worked in the industry 100 years ago. From a person-to-person business with the broker controlling all the information and access to trading, the industry has evolved into a complex and sometimes overwhelming world of products, services, trading systems, financial institutions, and information providers. Despite, or because of, the proliferation of financial information and news sources, clients need financial advisors now more than ever. Understanding the complexity of modern financial markets and products requires professional guidance.

Financial planning is now provided by brokerage firms, banks, insurance companies, independent advisors and certified public accountants. Even Internet firms provide boilerplate financial plans developed from questionnaires. Financial planning's reputation has been hurt lately because the planning process has been used to increase product sales instead of guiding clients to their objectives. This is particularly true among commission-based service providers. Those who have used the planning process to increase sales, however, are seldom able to maintain long-term careers in financial planning.

Personal financial services are one sector of the economy that will likely continue to grow and not be outsourced, if services are delivered with a "high touch" customized personal approach. If financial services are based on electronic access and packaged products and do not have personal consulting and advice, they will likely be vulnerable to outsourcing.

Financial advisors are finding they need increasingly specialized knowledge to understand the plethora of complex investments and successfully serve their clients' unique specific needs. They are also finding that learning skills in areas typically overlooked in business education, such as interpersonal communication and psychology, may help them better service their clients.

As in most industries, change is the only constant. The financial services industry will continue to evolve. Advisors and securities firms must do what human beings have always done — they must adapt to survive.

CHAPTER 2

The Changing Role of Financial Advisors

Evolving a Business of Executing Orders to Providing Comprehensive Financial Services

The role of financial advisors evolved in the 20th century in response to changes in the securities industry. As the U.S. economy gained strength over the last 100 years, and legal reforms were enacted, securities markets thrived and brokerage firms expanded across the country, offering innovative products and services to a growing number of investors.

Technology inalterably affected the securities industry, especially toward the end of the 20th century. Brokers benefited from increasing access to financial information, but their clients eventually gained access to the same information. Brokers used advancements in communications technology to execute their clients' trade orders, but the Internet later enabled investors to bypass brokers, using web-based systems to execute their trade orders.

Financial advisors adapted to these and other conditions as the nation, the industry, security firms and their clients changed throughout the 20th century. Financial advisors have had to play new roles, find new approaches and ways of doing business, and even adopt new names to describe their profession.

New Names

In the beginning of the 20th century, brokers were known as **customers men**, "men" being the operative word as there are no records of any women filling these positions. Customers men had a fairly-limited role. They chased down rumors and information for their clients, provided quotes, and executed their clients' buy and sell orders.

Customers men became **registered representatives** after reform legislation of the 1930s required brokers to become registered with the NASD, though their roles did not significantly change until the second half of the 20th century. By mid-century, securities exchanges, industry trade groups, regulatory agencies, and the U.S. Census Bureau all classified anyone licensed to sell securities of any kind as a registered representative, which is still used as the formal industry nomenclature today.

In the second half of the 20th century, the function of a registered representative changed considerably, and new terms developed to describe the profession. The growth of securities markets after World War II, and the increasing number of products and services developed by the securities industry, required registered representatives to play an increasingly advisory role with their clients. Investors needed their registered representatives to explain increasingly complex markets, investments, products and strategies. As registered representatives spent more time serving these needs, new titles emerged to describe specialized functions within the industry, and to elevate the general perception of the profession.

The title "financial advisor" arose to acknowledge the registered representatives' increasing role as a counselor to their client, as opposed to simply providing quotes and executing orders. Financial advisors also became known as account executives, investment advisors, wealth managers, financial planners, and many other names that were either fashionable at one time, or described different types of services provided by these professionals.

The customers men, who were little more than clerks, had become the registered representatives, a term that still suggested a purely functionary or bureaucrat role, which in turn became the modern financial advisors and account executives. These titles embodied their new roles as well-trained, management-level advisory professionals.

New Products

In the beginning of the 20th century, an investor could purchase stock in an individual company. Throughout the 20th century, new funds and investment vehicles were introduced, which greatly affected the role of the financial advisor. Clients required greater explanation and consultation to know which products were optimal for their investment goals. Financial advisors had to perform increasing amounts of research to keep informed on all the new products in order to be able to accurately advise their clients. Advisors also began to specialize in certain products in order to manage the growing quantities of information.

By the 1980s, there were a few index funds available representing the Standard & Poor's 500 index and Dow Jones average. Today, there are numerous Index funds, including NASDQ, Russell 100, Russell 500, Russell 1000, Wilshire and others. Exchange Traded Funds (ETFs) were introduced in the 1990s, and now there are ETFs for almost every industry, in addition to the general markets. Many special purpose funds were also developed as the securities industry matured, including concentrated portfolios, and funds focused on specific industries. Hedge funds were originally reserved only for very rich investors, but are now available to many investors, resulting in a fourfold increase in the number of hedge funds in the last decade.

In recent years, the rate at which new investment products were introduced has significantly increased. At the height of the tech boom, for example, mutual fund companies introduced perhaps 50 new tech and Internet mutual funds. The number of mutual funds has tripled in the last 20 years. Entirely new classes of mutual funds have been developed. Originally, mutual funds had A shares and up-front fees. Mutual funds then introduced B shares with no up-front fee, but with a 12B-1 charge each year for five to seven years, with a penalty charge if the shares were sold before the 12B-1 fee expired. Mutual funds then began to offer C shares with no withdrawal fee, and a one percent commission charge each year. Then there were D shares, which have no up-front fee, no 12B-1 fees, and no early withdrawal penalties, but have very large minimum investment requirements, sometimes as much as $1 million.

There has also been a dramatic increase in asset-based insurance products, as well as mortgages, direct corporate lending, Roth IRAs, simple retirement plans and a host of other investment products.

New Clients

Throughout the 20th century, financial advisors adapted not only to an increasing number of markets, products and services, and to changes in the roles they were required to play, but also had to manage significant changes in the kinds of clients they served, and the goals their clients pursued.

In the early part of the century, investors fell into three general categories. First and foremost were the very wealthy. People like John D. Rockefeller, J.P. Morgan, Andrew Mellon and the Knickerbocker family owned or controlled most companies, even if they were publicly traded. They ran the banks, oil companies, railroads and utility companies, as well as the investment trusts that allowed them to exercise control over entire industries. They invested and traded using inside information derived through personal relationships with others in their elite group. Frequently, their investing goal was to take control of companies or create pyramids of companies under investment trusts, which allowed them to maintain a controlling interest over several companies in the same sector, essentially forming industry monopolies.

President Theodore Roosevelt's anti-trust enforcement, and the 1911 lawsuit against Standard Oil, which resulted in a $29 million fine, influenced the behavior of the small group of very rich individuals who controlled much of the nation's wealth and many of its major companies.

Before the SEC required disclosure of any concentrated ownership in a company, large investors would accumulate a controlling interest in a company and then use their leverage to take over management. They often used an investment trust or other people's names to disguise the true extent of their ownership. After gaining control of a company, some of these investors operated ethically, and some used their monopoly power to drive competitors out of business, control prices, reduce wages, and engage in other questionable activities in pursuit of higher profits and greater industry control.

The financial advisors of this period, referred to as customers men or registered representatives, were used to execute buy and sell orders, provide quotes and chase down information and rumors, but had little advisory responsibility when serving these wealthy clients, who were primarily focused on controlling particular companies and industries, rather than maximizing investment returns.

The second major group of clients was the speculators. "Reminiscences of a Stock Operator," written by Edwin Lefevre, was first published in 1923 and still sells briskly today. In his book, Lefevre makes a distinction between investors and speculators. According to Lefevre, speculators' only objective was to make quick money. Speculators concentrated on small companies because they more were vulnerable to manipulation. It would not take a large amount of trading to push the stock price of a small company up or down. They also focused on companies that were not well known, so information about the company could be influenced by rumors and insider information. It was not unusual for speculators to start rumors in order to take advantage of the resulting shifts in a company's stock price.

The financial advisors of this time were also limited in their advisory duties when serving speculators, as these investors were interested in companies and industries that were vulnerable to manipulation, rather than those that promised the most significant growth and greatest overall returns.

The third major group of investors was comprised of people who bought large, well-known companies that paid generous dividends. In the early twentieth century, large companies frequently paid dividends that provided higher yields than the interest rates for bonds. Before long-term investing focused on earnings growth, a change that began in the 1920s, the goal of most investors was to maximize income. Bonds were the safest form of investment income. Income from dividends was considered to be riskier, so investors demanded dividend rates that were higher than the interest rates for bonds in order to justify the risk of owning common stock.

Because these investors valued dividend and interest returns above earnings potential, the advisory role of financial advisors was not as necessary as it became later in the century, when clients required Advisors' expertise and guidance to help them navigate the complex array of securities markets, investments and products.

New Laws and Regulations
While the Sherman Anti-Trust Act of 1890 was

enacted to control monopolistic trusts, enforcement of the Act had been limited almost exclusively to the prosecution of unions until Theodore Roosevelt became president after the assassination of William McKinley in September 1901. Roosevelt served as president until 1909 and aggressively enforced anti-trust laws throughout his terms in office, inciting legal action against a number of companies, and pushing new regulatory legislation through Congress.

New laws, regulations and rules implemented in the early 1930s also impacted the securities industry, and influenced the ways registered representatives behaved and worked with their clients. The discipline of stock analysis was also considered to be increasingly reliable as new laws were enacted to regulate the securities industry, including those requiring periodic company reporting and public disclosure. Analysts had more frequent, consistent and reliable information about companies. As a result, clients turned to their registered representatives for financial guidance, as the information they received was proven to be of greater accuracy and usefulness than in the past.

New Firms

After the stock market crash of 1929, there were a lot fewer clients and a lot fewer registered representatives. A great deal of wealth was lost in the crash. The public distrusted the securities markets, financial firms and their brokers. Even though the registered representatives had increasingly accurate and useful information about companies, the number of people investing in the stock market dropped considerably, and the reputation and livelihood of the registered representatives was imperiled.

The securities industry did not fully recover until the late 1940s, when the growth of the U.S. economy bolstered investors' confidence in the markets, and rising post-war employment and wages encouraged more individual investors to trade in securities. These new investors required even more guidance, information and customer service than those who came before them, opening new roles and markets for financial advisors.

Before the stock market crash, Charles Merrill was one of the few people who believed the markets were dangerously over valued. He advised people to sell their stocks and even closed his own brokerage firm. In 1940, Charlie Merrill joined his old partner, Edward Lynch, to open a new brokerage firm, Merrill Lynch. As the original partnership grew, and the company opened new offices and added new partners, the firm became Merrill Lynch, Pierce, Fenner and Bean, but continued to be known by its original name, Merrill Lynch.

Merrill Lynch focused on serving the increasing numbers of individual investors. The company opened offices in cities across the country and bought several local firms to expand their geographic reach. Other trading firms were growing in a similar manner. Goodbody, Harris Upman, Paine Webber and E.F. Hutton were taking on partners and opening new offices across the nation. Several regional firms were also developing, such as Dean Witter, which was expanding along the West Coast of the United States.

In 1945, Charlie Merrill took major steps to provide improved brokerage services to his clients. One innovation was the development of the first formal broker training program. Intensive broker training programs were quickly adopted by most securities firms. To recognize the role of brokers as highly-trained professionals, they were given a new title, account executive.

Many of the institutional firms that focused on investment banking and trading had also built significant securities research capabilities. Firms like Solomon Brothers, Goldman Sachs and a number of specialty boutique firms, such as Auerbach-Pollach, Mitchell Hutchinson, and Burnham Securities, supplied most of the institutional research.

The firms that focused on serving individual clients began to provide better securities research for their brokers and retail clients, though for many years, systems used by firms to transmit research among their brokers was inefficient and time-consuming. Research reports were frequently transmitted by teletype machines to the branch offices, which received the reports on mimeograph master sheets. The master sheets then had to be duplicated on mimeograph machines in the local offices, and the hard copies distributed to individual brokers. Although this slow and laborious process was the best firms had at the time to provide research to their clients, it was far more sophisticated than the previous method — soliciting advice from business associates, friends and family members.

New firms and new research methods gave financial advisors increasing authority, autonomy and expertise. Customers men had become specialized, well-informed, highly-trained, professional financial advisors, with nationwide networks of offices, access to valuable, proprietary research and the latitude to solicit clients from all social classes, including the middle-class and working class, from which came many of the new investors.

New Brokers

Brokers from longstanding, family-connected firms like Kidder Peabody and Smith Barney were known as "white shoe" brokers because of their elevated social status. These firms usually hired brokers from the same social class as their upscale clients. However, as securities firms expanded across the country and began catering to new individual investors from all classes of society, they increasingly hired talented young people without social connections or family wealth.

The role of the financial advisor changed markedly during this period, from that of a "white shoe" broker who cultivated social connections, appealing to small numbers of wealthy clientele, to that of a salesman who aggressively pursued large numbers of customers from all walks of life.

In the 1960s and 1970s, financial advisors were pressured to open a prescribed number of accounts per month. New brokers were sometimes required to open 10 new accounts each month. Financial advisors therefore spent a great deal of time soliciting new clients. At the time, brokers attracted clients primarily through educational seminars, or by simply cold-calling massive numbers of people. They were some of the few sales professionals who cold-called prospects at both their homes and businesses, sometimes late into the evening. Some advisors were placing over 100 calls a day. The role of the financial advisor changed once again, as the profession demanded brokers be adept salesmen as well as astute investment counselors.

New Sources of Information

In the early 20th century, brokerage offices were primarily located in major cities, with a concentration in New York. Most customers men were from wealthy or prestigious families. They belonged to the same clubs and social organizations as their customers, and acquired new clients largely through business, social and family contacts.

At the time, information about markets and companies was derived through personal contacts, not independent research. There was little if any securities research available for clients. Information was circulated by word of mouth, so access to information was limited to friends, family and business associates. This system for acquiring investment information hindered the role of financial advisors, as clients sought the advice of those in their social circle, rather than professional financial counselors.

Securities research was not recognized as a formal discipline until the Securities Act of 1933 and the publication in 1934 of Benjamin Graham and David Dodd's book, "Security Analysis," which was adopted by most business schools at the time to teach research methods. As securities research became a more sophisticated and specialized field, and the information generated was taken more seriously by investors, the role of financial advisors changed. The role of customers men, who simply executed trade orders, evolved into the role of a valued advisor with special knowledge of companies and markets derived through rigorously-tested analysis.

In the 1940s and '50s, brokers had control of most of the investment information. There was little financial news available through television or radio programs.

Television stations were few, and there was no cable TV. Evening news programs would carry a general statement on the activity of the markets, and maybe a few local interest stock quotes. Except for a few large cities, local newspapers carried a very short list of quotes, and the quotes were often the opening rotation prices of the previous day, rendering them effectively useless. The Wall Street Journal was informative, but arrived a day late. If someone wanted a current stock quote or a research report, they had to call their broker. There was no other source of investment information apart from stock market news letters, which were primarily written without any significant research, comprised mostly of passing observations and personal opinions, with little if any analysis. Brokers thrived because they controlled the information.

Even the brokers, however, were not that well informed. Most brokers did not engage in much in-depth reading or analysis. Their information came through a teletype machine, and was often posted on a clipboard in the office. Their historical research was based on the same mimeographed teletype messages, usually stored in a filing cabinet. If they could not find the teletype text they needed, there was no way to obtain another copy.

Most offices had Standard & Poor's company reports, but had no way to make copies for clients. Until the early 1960s, the only stock quote information was a ticker tape that ran across a screen in the front of the office. Clerks used blackboards to post recent prices on a limited list of local interest stocks. When electronic quote machines arrived in the mid-60s, up to four brokers shared one quote machine. This was not much of a problem, as the only information the machines could provide was stock quotes, volumes, earnings and a few other current numbers.

If investors wanted information, they would enter a brokerage office, sit in a row of customers' seats and watch the ticker tape. If they wanted information on specific stocks, they would see if the broker could obtain a research report or take notes from the Standard & Poor's company reports. These reports did not contain trading recommendations, and their information could be months or even a year out of date.

Because all communication to the home office was through teletype systems, brokers would not know if they had received confirmation that an order had been executed until it was sent to the teletype operator, matched with a hand-written order ticket, and finally returned to the broker. If it was a busy day or the teletype operator was on a break, the broker had no recourse but to wait. If it was a very busy day, trade confirmation might not be received by the broker until after the market had closed.

Because communication systems were not as dependable as they are now, it was not unusual for the entire system to fail. The only way to place orders was by phone. Incoming phone calls were so numerous that firms had rooms lined with wall phones. When the teletype machine went down, extra clerks, traders and anyone that knew how to take an order rushed to the phones to manage the incoming calls. Errors and delays were frequent. When these system failures took place, it was not unusual to get order confirmations a day or two after the order had been placed.

Because of the confusion, mistakes, arguments and temper outbursts, the phone walls were nicknamed "wailing walls" to describe the distress and disorder.

In the late 1960s and early '70s, securities firms began to provide broad-based research to their retail brokers. A new publication, The Institutional Investor, printed an annual "All American" list of the top institutional securities analysts in each industry. The All American list is still published today. While they were providing securities research, retail firms like Merrill Lynch were not yet focused on institutional clients, and therefore, as sophisticated as their research department were, they had no analysts on the Institutional Investor All American list. Their research may have been very good, but it had little authority or credibility.

All major securities firms, therefore, both retail and institutional, began to provide in-depth research to institutions in order to get an Institutional Investor All American rating. They needed the rating to ensure the reputation of their analysts and research departments. This led to a general improvement in the quality of research available to brokers, and in turn, their clients.

The desire to secure an All American rating led to an increase in analysts' salaries, as firms bid to hire All American analysts. The increase in salaries in turn attracted more highly-educated professionals to the securities industry, further bolstering the quality of research available to brokers and the general public. Biochemists from large pharmaceutical companies or marketing directors of major retail firms, for example, left their industries to become star securities analysts.

Through the 1950s and into the early '60s, professional analysts working at securities firms controlled most of the information available to the general public. In the 1960s and '70s, however, retail versions of investment products, previously available only to wealthy clients, were created to attract customers from the burgeoning middle class. These new investors were anxious to become better informed on the markets and the new securities products available to them.

The age of the informed consumer had begun. Fortune magazine became a bi-weekly publication, while Money, Worth and many other new publications provided investment information and advice for the first time directly to the general public. This trend continues to the present day, when financial magazines number in the dozens, book stores have entire departments devoted to investing, financial news television and cable networks are available at any time of the day or night, and investment Web sites proliferate on the Internet.

These revolutionary changes in the distribution of investment information dramatically impacted the role of financial advisors. Like medical doctors and other professionals, financial advisors lost control of the information their clients formerly required them to provide, and with it, a measure of control over their profession. The public no longer viewed most professionals as the sole keepers of exclusive knowledge. Everyone could easily access much of the information that used to require years of education and experience to obtain. Financial advisors and other professionals were increasingly considered to be service providers, rather than treasured conduits of specialized expertise.

Once regarded as oracles of the markets, with special

access to investment secrets and insights, brokers have since lost control of information and direct access to executing transactions in the market. Those advisors who have not changed have began to resemble the customers men of the early 20th century, executing trade orders for their clients, who receive their information and advice elsewhere. Today's securities business demands that successful advisors must develop new skills to be able to provide broader and more sophisticated services to deal with investors' more complex investment needs.

There is an interesting parallel between clients and their brokers and patients and their doctors. Up through the 1930s and '40s, outside of the largest cities, most doctors were general practitioners. They treated their clients for most of their health needs. They set bones, did all but the major surgeries, delivered babies, and treated children, adults and the elderly.

Only a few decades ago, most people knew the names of only a few drugs, such as penicillin, aspirin and sulfur. Doctors wrote prescriptions in Latin, and frequently the pharmacist couldn't read the doctors handwriting and had to call them to be sure of what was prescribed. No one had yet heard about generic substitutes. To most people, penicillin was the generic name for antibiotics, just as Xerox is now the accepted name for copying.

The instructions for taking drugs were normally communicated orally by the doctor or the pharmacist. It was not unusual for the two to give different instructions depending on what they had last read. There were no written details included for the patient regarding the drug, its dosage or side effects. Many pharmacies not only carried a limited number of drugs, they frequently carried a very small stock. It was not unusual for a pharmacy to have to place an order for a drug and for the patient to have to wait a day or more to come back to pick up a prescription.

People only knew about a few ailments and knew that there was little that could be done about many of them, such as polio, arthritis, cancer, or heart disease. Frequently, doctors did not even describe diseases by their formal names. If a person was suspected of having a virus, they were usually told they had a bug that would probably go away in a few days. If a person wanted more information, they could go to the bookstore, but about the only book available on health was the medical encyclopedia. The book was technical and very difficult for lay people to understand. In many cases, even medical professionals had limited knowledge of most diseases and ailments.

Doctors controlled all of the information. What little they told patients during the office visit was all the information patients received. Patients probably got more information secondhand, in conversations with family and friends, and the information was often incomplete or incorrect.

Most doctors had individual practices, and there was limited health insurance so people paid whatever the doctors charged. If people were seriously sick, they were often sent to big-city hospitals for treatment. Many cities only had one hospital. Mid-sized cities had maybe two or three hospitals, normally a general hospital and a hospital sponsored and run by a religious order.

Investors were in a similar position. Just as doctors controlled medical information, stockbrokers controlled most financial information.

New Competition

Financial advisors have also had to manage new competition from many sources. A proliferation of product delivery channels has emerged in the securities industry. Originally, only brokerage offices were able to buy and sell securities, just as insurance companies were exclusively licensed to sell insurance, trust departments in banks provided trust services, attorneys managed estate planning and accountants handled tax preparation and financial planning.

These industries have since evolved into a multiple product and service delivery model. Each channel now competes to provide the same products and services to the same clients. Traditional brokerage firms now offer most financial services except tax preparation and legal representation. Independent financial planners also deliver many of the same products and services. Trust departments are becoming asset management firms. Tax consultancies are offering financial advisory services. H&R Block, for example, which once focused entirely on tax preparation, is now offering investment services. Discount firms and online brokerages are also providing a broader range of services, frequently partnering with other businesses to deliver additional products and services. Schwab, for example, refers clients to affiliated financial planners and investment advisors, while retaining the trade execution business. Online brokerage firms are even offering on-line banking and low-price life insurance.

A recent entrant in the market is the independent entity. This is usually a brokerage operation, which may be part of a traditional brokerage firm, bank or insurance company, or may be a hybrid company such as Raymond

James. The planners, brokers, or whatever they are called are actually independent contractors. Much like in a franchise operation, these brokers receive resources and support, including regulatory compliance, from a parent company, but are responsible for their expenses, and must provide a fee to the parent company, much like a franchisee.

Brokers have traditionally been paid for their services from commissions earned on trades. Recently, however, clients have preferred to retain a broker to provide investment and financial planning advice, paying them under a similar fee-for-service system as that used by accountants and attorneys. Many firms in the securities and financial planning industry now offer clients the choice of paying sales commissions or service fees.

Increasing competition and the introduction of the fee-for-service model significantly affected the role of the financial advisor. Some financial advisors have become independent agents in order to partner with other professionals to offer more products. The fee-for-service model spurred brokers to focus less on generating trading commissions and more on providing other kinds of services to their clients, such as financial planning, asset allocation, insurance consultation and investment manager selection.

New Approaches

Financial advisors have developed new approaches in response to the vast changes in the securities industry. The most notable trend is for financial advisors to become independent operators, usually working under a larger company like Raymond James, Linsco Private

Ledger and other similar firms. The independent sector started slowly, but each year captures a greater percentage of the industry's business.

As competition increased, financial advisors no longer wanted to be limited in the products and services they could provide their clients. As independent operators, they could offer a wide range of products and services, partner with whomever they liked, use whichever fee structure best fit their business, and in general experienced the benefits and satisfaction of running their business as they saw fit.

Independent financial advisors could also be more selective in their choice of clients. Brokerage companies traditionally insisted their new brokers meet a quota, opening a certain number of accounts per month. This model was intended to increase revenues for the parent company, but it frequently resulted in an inefficient use of brokers' resources. Financial advisors found they were spending an inordinate amount of time opening and servicing unproductive accounts, leaving less time for potentially lucrative clients.

Becoming independent operators freed financial advisors from quotas, allowing them to more efficiently use their resources and limit their costs. Financial advisors have found that better serving more lucrative clients, while investing fewer resources in opening potentially unproductive accounts, has significantly increased their profits.

The 1980s saw the end of the traditional markets as they had existed for over 100 years. An entirely new business model was introduced, altering the relationship between investors and financial advisors. In many ways, it was a very good decade for investors, advisors and advisory firms. The value of American securities mushroomed and financial advisors saw their revenues increase commensurately. However, it was also during this period that investors gained greater access to financial information, and were able to execute securities transactions through a variety of new channels, including discount and on-line brokerages. Financial advisors did not swiftly react to these changes because their revenues were growing and record profits were being accrued.

The 1990s brought changes to the securities industry that eclipsed even those that came in the previous decade. Information technology and the Internet inalterably affected the securities industry. Online financial information, account management and trade execution rendered obsolete many of the services traditionally delivered by large brokerage firms. Confident young entrepreneurs established new financial companies in cyberspace. Brick and mortar securities firms were slow to react to and compete with the Internet newcomers. Those who adapted to the new business environment and incorporated use of the Internet proved the most successful. Financial advisors who embraced new techniques and technologies thrived in the new securities marketplace.

The New Advisor

At one time, securities firms measured their brokers by the number of accounts they opened. Firms believed that clients' needs were much the same and encouraged their brokers to open as many accounts as possible. Many new financial advisors today are still required to open a minimum number of accounts each month for the first two to five years they are in the business. Larger accounts are preferable, but many financial services companies still put a higher premium on the number of accounts opened rather than the size of those accounts or an estimation of the resources required to service them.

Financial advisors typically spend a couple of hours meeting with their good clients each quarter, and 30 minutes in the each of the other eight months talking with them, which adds up to 12 hours each year. A typical American working year is about 2,000 hours. At 12 hours a year per client, there is a limit to how many clients an advisor can service. Assuming an advisor works evenings and weekends to do research and prepare presentations, and spends every 8-5 working day servicing clients, this works out to a maximum of 167 clients an advisor can adequately service at one time.

However, financial advisors are often expected to manage several hundred or even 1,000 or more accounts simultaneously. Even financial advisors who have become successful or independent operators often strive to continually open new accounts, having been trained and indoctrinated to do so throughout their careers.

Financial advisors are increasingly finding, however, that they cannot possibly spend enough time with each account to provide quality service. In addition, they usually do not have enough expertise in every financial discipline to meet the diverse needs of a large number of clients. Seldom can a single advisor have all the skills needed to service every client's unique requirements.

Financial advisors are also aware that a single investment solution is no longer appropriate for all investors. Previously, when a financial advisor identified an attractive security, they offered it to all their clients. It was a product-driven industry; now it is client-driven. Each client must be seen as an unique investor, with distinct needs that require specialized skills and expertise.

To thrive in today's securities environment, a financial advisor should therefore be a specialist who seeks clients that need their distinct skills. They must know what they do well and find clients that need what they do. They must define and communicate their value proposition: what makes them uniquely valuable to a distinct kind of client.

Financial advisors should also work strategically with other specialists. An emerging trend is for independent financial advisors and other professionals to form teams of specialists in order to provide greater expertise and services to clients with diverse needs.

Financial advisors are no longer able to attract and retain clients simply by being available to them and offering relatively knowledgeable investment advice. Investors can execute trade orders any time over the Internet and access more financial information than financial advisors have available through their firms.

The securities industry requires professional advisors who can provide guidance not only on a variety of investments, but also on a variety of issues their clients experience. Clients want financial advisors that are skilled at solving problems. They want financial planners to create a more comprehensive framework for their investments, one that takes into account their needs, experiences, desires and passions. Clients increasingly regard financial advisors as conduits for more than just financial information. They look to financial advisors as a source of professional relationships, referrals, and even personal advice.

In the 20th century, *customers men* became *registered representatives*, who became *financial advisors*. In the 21st century, financial advisors have become more than just securities specialists. They have become life specialists, and so deserve a new title — *Life Advisors*.

CHAPTER 3

The New Customer Service Model

Servicing Both the Client and Their Assets, Exceeding Their Expectations

Financial advisors must understand customer service to be successful. This may seem like common sense, but financial advisors have not always been trained to focus on customer service. Brokers have traditionally been required to open increasing numbers of new accounts at the expense of servicing current accounts. The new customer service model recognizes that providing excellent customer service not only leads to an increase in clients, but more importantly, attracts the right clients. Customer service is about pleasing clients, but it also involves account management: how efficiently professional advisors service their customers. The financial advisor must meet the client's needs by providing outstanding service and skills, but the client must also meet the financial advisor's needs: the customer must need the financial advisor's particular skills. The financial advisor must choose the right clients in order to successfully and efficiently service them.

Managing and exceeding customer services expectations can have a "multiplier effect" that enhances and promotes the reputation of the financial advisor. By establishing a correct value statement that reflects the relationship between their skills and their target market, financial advisors can attract and satisfy the right kinds of clients. Financial advisors must also be able to influence the behavior of their clients in order to provide superior customer service, and can improve their ability to do so through the use of reciprocity, social proof, authority, likeability, scarcity and commitment. Financial advisors can also benefit by looking outside their industry for parallel examples in other trades and practices, such as the medical profession.

The Expectation Game

Customer service is about expectations. If clients expect average service, then anything better will impress them. If they expect excellent service, anything less will disappoint them. Great customer service is often unexpected customer service. Customers today expect such meager service that they are often delighted if a firm simply adheres to standard business practices, while a small increase in customer service can make a disproportionate impression on clients. This increase in customer service often requires little investment on the part of the service provider, or represents an expense that is more than balanced by their fees.

The New Customer Service Model

In our presentations to financial advisors, we often ask them to describe the customer service that has most impressed them. When asked to provide examples of superior customer service, they most often respond with a story in which a marginal increase in customer service made a big impact on them. They will recount how their car dealership drove them back home or to work after they brought their car in for service. Even if they drive a luxury car that costs upward of $75,000, they are delighted to be driven to work in a van with four other customers. Or they may describe a hotel doorman who greeted them with a big smile or asked how they are doing. This is, of course, the doorman's job, to greet the hotel's guests with enthusiasm. Yet, because people have such low customer service expectations, they are mightily impressed by the doorman's behavior. Financial advisors have even mentioned incidents when they returned a defective product and received a new one in exchange. This level of service should be expected, yet people find it surprising when they are treated fairly, with common decency or according to standard business practices. Clients today expect poor customer service because they aren't used to receiving anything better. The level of customer service may in fact be at its lowest point in modern history.

There are exceptions, of course. A few companies provide consistently superb service. The Ritz-Carlton chain of hotels, for example, generally receives very high marks on many aspects of their customer service. Nordstrom department stores seem to get the customer service gold medal for retailing. Unfortunately, these examples are so rare as to indicate there are only a few firms in the United States that make any concerted effort to provide outstanding customer service.

The St. Regis Resort hotel in Dana Point is another operation that profits from unexpected customer service. A story we frequently hear involves someone checking into the hotel for a sales meeting. It happens that the St. Regis hotel competes with one of the flagship hotels in the Ritz-Carlton chain, the Ritz-Carlton at Laguna Niguel. Although the St. Regis is in the general vicinity of the Ritz-Carlton, it is at a severe disadvantage. The Ritz-Carlton is on one of the more beautiful beaches in Southern California, while the St. Regis is further inland so that you can't even see the beach from the hotel.

The St. Regis is a beautiful property with all the luxurious amenities of a world-class resort, except of course, a location on a beautiful beach. As the story goes, a customer checks into their room, throws all their clothes on the bed, and leaves to go jogging, to the beach, or to dinner. When they return, they find to their dismay that their clothes appear to have been stolen, as they are no longer lying on the bed where they left them. They often call hotel security at this point, and are informed by the security officer, who frequently receives this kind of call, that they should look in the room's closet, where all their clothes are neatly pressed and folded.

Another example involves a purchase made at a department store. The customer bought some shoes from the store and before they even took them out of the box, their six-month-old Labrador retriever puppy ate the left shoe. The customer sheepishly returns to the department store and asks the sales clerk if it is possible to buy only a left shoe. The clerk asks what happened and when the customer recounts the story of the puppy, the clerk says the store would be happy to send them a new pair at no charge. As impressive as this seems, it is even more impressive if you ask people which store they think extended this service. This scenario has been posed to thousands of people over the years, and in our experience, they always believe it could only be Nordstrom. Only once did someone in an audience mention another high-end department store, but the other people in the audience immediately said it couldn't be that store and that it had to be Nordstrom. This kind of reputation is priceless, and certainly worth the customer service investments Nordstrom has made over the years.

The Multiplier Effect

The audience's near universal agreement that Nordstrom provides the best retail service exemplifies what might be called the "multiplier effect" of good customer service. When asked to volunteer stories of impressive customer service, people are always very enthusiastic to tell them, as if they can't wait to share them with everyone else. When a business provides exceptional service, the customer is pleased, of course, and likely to return to that business, but they are also likely to tell their friends, family and associates.

The business creates an image, a presence in the marketplace that is identified with good customer service. The same can be said of bad customer service. People are eager to tell the world about it. In the restaurant industry, for example, it is said that a customer who enjoys their meal will tell six people, but the dissatisfied customer will tell 12. That is the multiplier effect, and it can have a profound impact on your business.

After we ask financial advisors to tell us their customer service experiences, we usually tell them that we are going to return in 90 days and give the same presentation again. However, this time, they're not going to be the audience, their clients are. We challenge them figure out what they could possibly do to cause their client to tell us about their outstanding service. In almost every case, the surprising result is that what the financial advisors propose to do for their clients has nothing to do with financial services.

Imagine the multiplier effect's impact on a financial advisor's business if every one of their most important clients was so impressed with their customer service that they could not wait to tell everyone they met about it. There is probably nothing a financial advisor could do that would be more effective to promote their business to the community, and improve their professional reputation.

There is a story we've heard about a financial advisor who had a birthday party for a wealthy widowed client. The advisor told her to invite six of her friends, and that he would take them all to his club for lunch. Of course, the wealthy widow's friends were also wealthy. After the lunch party, the widow's friends remarked, "My financial advisor doesn't take me out to lunch on my birthday!" What happened next is predictable. Several of the wealthy client's friends became his clients as well.

The Right Client

Why don't more companies focus on improving their customer service? Perhaps they forget that the purpose of a business is to attract and retain customers, and not to squeeze the maximum amount of profit from each customer transaction. Companies have a tendency to skimp on relatively inexpensive customer service efforts that could generate much greater returns in the future. This short-sightedness was described many years ago in Ted Levitt's breakthrough book, "Marketing Myopia."

Investment professionals are very good at finding customers. Financial advisors have evolved into account generating machines, in part because they have been trained to open as many accounts as possible, instead of being taught to target the right account. Firms judged and rewarded brokers based on the number of accounts they opened, rather than the quality of the accounts they maintained. If you are entirely focused on opening new accounts, the service your existing accounts receive is bound to suffer.

The financial services industry has changed significantly in recent years, yet this attitude is still pervasive. "Open accounts" is the sales mantra of the financial services industry. Our research reveals that 18 percent of a typical financial advisor's clients are responsible for 80 percent of their business. This is not surprising, as the "80/20 rule" applies to many of life's relationships. What is surprising is the rest of the distribution. While 22 percent of a typical financial advisor's clients are responsible for 16 percent of their business, a whopping 60 percent of clients account for only four percent of their business.

This 60/4 relationship causes most financial advisors to inefficiently manage their accounts. Sixty percent of a financial advisor's clients provide only four percent of their business, but those clients still require a great deal of the time the advisor devotes to customer service. If an advisor devotes the same amount of time to each client, this results in four percent of their business devouring 60 percent of their customer service time. Remember, 40 percent of their clients contribute 96 percent of their income. Instead of lavishing their customer service efforts on the minority of their clients that provide 96 percent of their income, their time, energy and focus are diluted servicing vastly unproductive accounts.

Even if financial advisors became aware of these statistics, it is still hard for any professional to accept that a significant majority of their customers contributes almost nothing to their business, and even more difficult to act on the proposition that they should jettison most of the clients. Even when financial advisors implement a program to drop unproductive accounts, they very often replace them with other unproductive accounts.

In order to optimize their client service relationships, financial advisors have to do more than drop existing accounts; they have to stop opening the wrong accounts in the future. Unfortunately, many advisors are addicted to new accounts. If they used programs to screen for the right accounts, they could spend less time to produce more revenue.

How do you determine what the right accounts are? First, you have to define what you mean by the "right" accounts. The "right" client is not necessarily the most affluent. There is much written in the financial media today about affluent accounts and the new value-added services financial professionals are creating for "high-net worth" individuals. Unfortunately, few people take the time to find out how many of these wealthy clients actually exist.

Studies vary, though a reasonable estimate would suggest there are approximately three million people in the United States who have investable assets, excluding their home, of one million dollars or more. Statistics also indicate there are at least one million financial advisory professionals and planners, including those in wire house brokerages, regional brokerages, banks, trust departments and insurance companies. This results in a ratio of three wealthy clients for each financial advisor. This is an average, of course, and depends on how you define "wealthy," but it certainly suggests most financial advisors will have to extend their definition of the "right" client to include people who aren't necessarily affluent by this definition.

What is the "right" client? We asked this question to over 100 of the most successful people we knew in the financial services industry. We got many different answers, but two characteristics stood out. A great client was someone who needed the particular excellence of the financial advisor, and was someone who took their advice. There were many other qualities mentioned, such as friendship, intelligence, decisiveness, and even fun, but it was clear the most important attributes of a great client was that they really needed that particular advisor, and followed their advice.

Now we face a difficult question — what are we good at? Financial advisors are not all good at the same things. A great client to one may be the worst client to another. One way to answer this question, to determine what we're good at, is to examine how we currently meet the needs of our best clients. What skills are we employing that help us satisfy those needs? If it is difficult to identify your particular skills, it might be useful to ask your clients what they consider to be your strengths and weaknesses.

The Value Statement

Many years ago, an old friend, Nick Murray, suggested financial professionals should have what he referred to as a *value statement*, a one or two sentence description that answers the question, "What do you do?" Professionals are constantly asked this question at business and social gatherings, yet their responses rarely communicate their true value. The answer to this question, the value statement, should define what they do and what kinds of clients they can best serve. The value statement identifies their target market and the clients that meet their marketing objectives. In other words, it is directed at the right clients.

Remember, the question you are trying to answer is, "What do I do?" not "Who am I?" Stating you are a financial advisor at XYZ firm answers the wrong question. Your response should indicate exactly what you are good at, providing enough information for the listener to assess whether or not they would consider using your services.

Nick Murray first described the concept of a value statement to us, so let's look at the value statement Nick created for himself over 12 years ago: "I am the intergenerational, global advisor to some of the most important people in this community." It is a mouthful, but also a pretty interesting statement of value. It is not for everyone, but it does have some useful descriptive properties for Nick.

First, what does "intergenerational" mean? We think it is one of the most important words in a financial advisor's vocabulary. The idea of taking care of an entire family's financial needs has some very positive connotations. Maintaining business relationships with several generations of the same family can greatly increase a financial advisor's potential number of million-dollar accounts, if you include an entire family. It also makes it more difficult for assets to leave when a death occurs, as the one who inherits the money will already be a client.

Secondly, Nick identifies himself as a global advisor. This is a pretty impressive sounding title, but most financial advisors use domestic and international account managers, so it's easy to justifiably include reference to "global" activities in your value statement. Global also means that the advisor takes care of all of their needs.

The third part of Nick's value statement is also very interesting: he indicates he is an advisor to some of the most important people in the community. Not the wealthiest, but the most important. What does he mean by that? Importance, of course, is subjective. Nick lets the listener decide if they are a member of one of the most important families in the community. He does, however, give the listener the impression that if they are not, he is the wrong advisor for them. In this way, Nick facilitates a self-selection process that helps screen potential clients, resulting in higher-quality accounts and a more efficient use of his customer service time.

If I worked in Silicon Valley, I might use the value statement, "I help one-stock multimillionaires diversify their assets." That would be a good value statement in an area where so many individuals meet that description.

Becoming a Life Advisor

If I was a one-stock multimillionaire who met you at a party, I might want to get to know you professionally if you provided that value statement.

At a workshop in New York, brokers who had just completed their first full year in production were brought back to the home office for some advanced training, to get reacquainted with each other, and to share best practices. Early in the workshop, we called on a number of people and asked: "What do you do?" The answers were predictable. One broker replied that he was a financial advisor for the ABC firm. Another said he was a "wealth manager," a fashionable term these days, to which we replied that a homeless person with nothing in their pockets probably needs a wealth manager more than anyone. Was that the kind of client he was looking for?

Then, one of the younger brokers said his value statement was, "I help people with $100 million or more optimize the asset and liability side of their balance sheet." We almost fell over when he said that, but we looked him in the eye and said, "You do what?" He repeated the same value statement. We then asked him, "How many accounts do you have?" "Seven," he replied. Then we asked him how many assets his seven clients had and he said they had $2.4 billion in assets. We were shocked because we had never run across anyone like this. We asked the young man if he would take a $50 million account, and he said he would definitely not. Then we asked if he would take both of us as clients, perhaps in a joint account arrangement, if we each had $50 million. He replied, "What is it about a $100 million minimum that you don't understand?"

There are an endless variety of value statements.

Find the one that fits you. If you don't like the market your value statement targets, then change it. Be sure, however, that you have the necessary skills required to deliver on your value statement. Most often, you will need to get some new skills to go with a new value statement. Avoid clients who require skills you don't possess, unless you plan to add those skills immediately.

The goal is to posses the skills necessary to provide outstanding service to the clients who meet your criteria. For example, there are many skills a financial advisor would need to service a one-stock multimillionaire. They would have to know about collars, forward sales, applicable securities regulations, competitive restricted lending and other issues. Once you determine your value statement and the market you are going after, you must add any skills necessary to implement superb customer service for that market.

Get a tape recorder and practice your value statement repeatedly until you feel absolutely comfortable with it. Say it to your spouse or significant other and see what they think. Test it against your skill set and make sure you are capable of delivering everything your value statement promises. Be sure it is targeted at the clients you are trying to attract. Continually hone your value statement. The answer to the question, "What are we good at?" is always evolving. Reassess your value statement regularly, and be sure it communicates your skills to your desired market.

Remember, two characteristics stood out when we asked people in the financial services industry, "What constitutes a great client?" According to their responses, a great client was someone who needed their skills, and someone who took their advice. It may seem irrational for a client to pay a professional for their advice and then ignore it, but it happens all the time, and can be frustrating for everyone involved. The financial advisor is unable to do their best for their client, and the client may not be seeing the returns they expected on their investments. When the client doesn't follow the financial advisor's directives, everyone loses.

Some people don't follow their doctor's advice, their lawyer's advice or their financial advisor's advice. In most cases, they have disastrous results and frequently blame their doctor, lawyer or advisor. People who will not follow their advisor's advice will most likely have poor results, make the advisor's life miserable and disparage their advisor to their friends.

How do financial advisors get their clients to follow their instructions? How does anyone get anyone to do what they want? We have studied these questions in great depth and have found the answers lie in psychology. In all our training as financial advisors, we received a fair amount of instruction in finance, but almost no training in psychology or interpersonal skills, which are fundamental to the profession.

Most of the sales training financial advisors are still receiving are closing tactics. They are taught to ask for the sale several times in a presentation. These are really modified strong-arm tactics that result in buyer's remorse. These sales methods do not build confidence and trust with clients.

Financial advisors must be able to influence people's behavior, yet most have never received any information or instruction on the subject. There are many sources of information on the subject of influence, but most are not pertinent to the role of the financial advisor, and none are found in standard business publications. The concept of interpersonal influence rarely makes the pages of Barron's, and is nowhere to be found in David Dodd and Benjamin Graham's books.

Financial advisors should stop reading Barron's and start reading psychology books. The best book to start with is Dr. Robert Cialdini's "Influence: The Psychology of Persuasion." Cialdini's work is by far the most helpful we have found on the subject of influence. His model is rather simple, and can be applied to financial advisors. His theories can help financial advisors be more influential, and can also help them attract the right clients.

In his work, Cialdini states there are six concepts that can be used to influence people. We often ask attendees of our workshops to try to name the six concepts, and to date no group has ever gotten more than two of them, again illustrating that our profession's most important skills have been entirely omitted from our formal education.

Reciprocity

The first Cialdini concept vital to influencing others is reciprocity. We are all familiar with the idea, but few of us realize how effective reciprocity is in building important relationships. It is such an important concept that we believe every financial advisor should subscribe to the dictum, "Do something wonderful for someone every single day of your life." We often tell our workshop audiences that this is the most important concept we will teach them all day.

Doing wonderful things for people on a daily basis is

123

like making deposits in a "Bank Account of Life." After a while, you will see the value of those deposits increase, and you will eventually receive much more than you have put into the account. You will realize that not only is it easy to do wonderful things for other people, but it also makes you feel pretty good, even if your motive originally was to strengthen and build relationships.

An example of reciprocity in the securities industry comes from many years ago, when one of us was the director of marketing at a major Wall Street firm. One day, we received a phone call from a friend who had a 22-year-old son. The friend said he had a very important favor to ask, one of the most important requests he had ever made. He said he wanted to get his son a job as an investment banker. This was 1980, when the whole world wanted to become investment bankers. Although his son graduated from a very fine university, it was not one from which a great number of students were recruited by Wall Street firms.

We told the friend we weren't sure his son was good enough to become an investment banker (a dumb thing to say, but we were young), but we would see what we could do. As it turned out, we got lucky and the son was hired as an investment banker trainee. Every day for the next 75 days the friend called to ask the same question, "What can I do to pay you back for helping me and my son?" On the 75th day, we told him to stop calling.

That friend has been of invaluable assistance over the last twenty-four years. We have referred business to each other and done many other wonderful favors for each other. His son has also become a friend and today he is a very successful banker in Silicon Valley. This was a valuable lesson: sometimes it is more powerful to do something for an individual's child or loved one than it is to do something directly for that individual.

Never hesitate to help people's children. Those people and their children will pay you back for a long time. There are many things you can do for people's children: coach their athletic teams, talk to them about your profession, higher them as interns, find them jobs, and so forth. Be creative. We have been responsible for dozens of sons and daughters of friends getting jobs or introductions at Wall Street firms. Our bank accounts keep growing, but they have often grown twice as quickly by doing generous favors for people's loved ones. This is what reciprocity is all about. Certainly, there are some ungrateful people in the world who will try to take advantage of you, but they are few and far between.

Social Proof

The second technique to influence other people is something Cialdini calls social proof, which can be described as the tendency for people to do business with those who do business with other people like them. People want to be part of a group they perceive to be similar to them. If your other clients are people like them, they want to be part of that group. It's also true that people want to be part of a group of people they perceive to be better than them. If your clients are more successful than they are, they also want to be part of that group. Either way, social proof entices people to want to be your clients.

It is instructive to examine how the concept of social

proof applies to Nick Murray's original value statement. "I am the intergenerational, global advisor to some of the most important families in this community," Nick said. "The most important families in this community" was Nick's way of invoking social proof, signaling to the listener that they would or should belong to this elite group. This plays to the listener's recognition of their own importance in the community. If the listener believes they are not a member of one of the most important families, it leverages their desire to ascend to a higher status group.

Another illustration of social proof can be found in the example of the birthday party provided earlier in this chapter. A financial advisor has a birthday party for a wealthy widowed client, and asks her to invite six of her friends. Why does the widow client only invite other affluent widows to the party? Social proof.

Social proof serves as a credential, a statement of recommendation. A value statement should use social proof to entice the listener, to make them think, "If people I am similar to use this particular Advisor, they must be good at serving those kinds of people, so they would be good at serving me."

Suppose someone approached you and said they wanted to open a $100 million account with you because you were highly recommended to them. Before they did, however, they wanted to know how many other $100 million accounts you have. If you had none and indicated as much, they might ask, "How many $50 million accounts do you have?" If you had none and answered truthfully, they might give you a $100,000 to invest. In this example, you failed the test of social proof.

Let us examine what would have happened if the individual had asked the same question to the young broker mentioned earlier in the chapter whose value statement was, "I help people with $100 million or more optimize their assets and liabilities." When asked, "How many $100 million accounts do you have," the young man may have replied, "All my accounts have at least $100 million. I won't deal with anyone who has less. As a matter of fact, my average client has $400 million." In this case, the individual would probably have given him $100 million, because he used social proof to earn credibility and entice the client.

Authority

The next important attribute in the world of influence is authority. What gives you the right to tell anyone anything? Why should anyone listen to you? When we give keynote addresses at conferences, we are always introduced with much fanfare and a reiteration of our accomplishments, titles, awards, degrees and so forth. This is all done to establish our authority with the audience. These are the credentials that give us the right to speak to our audience as an expert.

You have to establish your authority. In the United States, authority is often established through the use of letters like Ph.D., MBA, CLU, CFP, CFA, and M.D. Do you have any letters? If not, you should get some and make sure the whole world knows you have them. They are essential to establishing your authority.

Authority makes anything you say more meaningful. It is one of the most important concepts to get your clients to listen to you and act on your advice. As an example, imagine having breakfast with your best friend, who is a golf instructor. You mention to him that you have been experiencing a sharp pain in your left leg, which is especially acute in the morning and after you have been sitting for an extended period. In response, he says, "I think you should amputate your leg."

You would probably be somewhat shocked by his suggestion, and most likely wouldn't race out to schedule an amputation. Now assume your best friend is not a golf instructor but chief oncologist at a well-respected hospital. Now how do you feel about his suggestion? His position of authority is represented by not only the letters M.D., but additionally the fact that he is board certified in oncology, which changes the way you react to his advice. The same is true of wealthy people reacting to you. On what do you base your authority? What are your letters?

Likeability

One of the most obvious attributes for influencing people is being liked. People in general only go out of their way to do things for people they like. If someone doesn't like you, they may ignore you or even try to hurt you. We often tell financial advisors to only deal with people they like, and who like them. This not only enhances your ability to influence your clients, but also helps improve your overall job satisfaction. It only makes sense that everyone is happier when they are surrounded by people who like them.

We have probably all met people we liked to be around, who made us feel good to be in their presence. Other people seem to suck the energy right out of us. It is best in business and in life to avoid "energy vampires" at almost any cost. We have heard countless stories of financial advisors who dropped their largest clients because they couldn't stand dealing with them. Even if they suffered a short-term loss of revenue, most of these advisors were much happier, and went on to see substantial increases in their productivity.

Do business with people you like and who like you. It is more productive, enjoyable, and rewarding. Social proof suggests that people gravitate to others like them, and therefore the people you like the most will more than likely surround themselves with those who like you.

Scarcity

The fifth attribute that can help influence people is scarcity. People want what they can't have. The scarcer something is, the more people will seek to obtain it. The most obvious examples are collectibles, such as art, furniture, or sports memorabilia. Stories of $50 million paintings, $1 million desks, and $500,000 baseball cards are routinely reported, revealing just how much people will pay for something they consider to be scarce. Even when something has a specific value attached to it, like the ticket price of a sporting event or concert, its value can escalate as it becomes scarce due to excess demand.

Scarcity creates value. If your services are considered to be a scarce commodity, then people will want them even more. The dynamic of scarcity is as old as the law of supply and demand. The rarer something is perceived to be, the more valuable it is. Diamonds are an interesting example. Though plentiful, diamonds are perceived to be rare, and are therefore valuable. Due to artificial manipulation, the world's supply of diamonds far exceeds the amount in circulation, which is tightly controlled by diamond cartels in order to increase the perceived scarcity, and therefore the sales price, of diamonds.

Scarcity implies quality. The "best" trial lawyers, surgeons, and money managers are those considered to be the most sought after, and are therefore the most difficult to obtain. The scarcer your services are perceived to be, the higher quality they will also be perceived to have.

It is instructive to review the Nick Murray value statement one more time: "I am the intergenerational, global advisor to the most important families in this community." This statement communicates Nick's value, quality and scarcity. If you are only available to a chosen few, then you are not available to everyone else, and that suggests your services are scarce and desirable.

Consider the example presented earlier of the young broker who would only deal with $100 million accounts. Do you think he has created the perception of scarcity? To such a great extent that someone with $75 million would beat a path to his door trying to get him to handle their account.

Scarcity is a very important concept when attempting to influence people, especially when you want them to act quickly. If a customer knows something is rare and they have a limited amount of time to make a decision before someone else gets it, they will be driven even harder to obtain it themselves as quickly as possible. When a sales-person tells you, "There is only one left and this is your last chance to get one," it can have a powerful effect on your desire to purchase whatever they are selling.

Commitment

The sixth and final quality you can use to persuade people is commitment. Financial advisors are not always good at asking their clients for commitments. Most people aren't good at it because they are hindered by their fear of failure. We are afraid to ask people for commitments because we are afraid they will turn us down. When financial advisors were taught to open every account they could find, they were often afraid to ask their prospects for commitments due to a fear the prospect would refuse, and this would end the relationship. One could ask, "What relationship?" however, since without some form of commitment, a relationship does not truly exist.

Once a commitment has been made, though, a relationship is created, even with perfect strangers. Imagine yourself waiting on a long line at the checkout stand of a supermarket. The person in front of you asks you to save their place in line while they retrieve another item. You protect their place because you gave a commitment. We fulfill commitments like this all the time. Once someone gives a commitment, they generally follow through with whatever they have committed to do.

The "second chance" dynamic is another aspect of the commitment principle. When someone feels committed to helping another person, and that person asks for perhaps too much assistance, and is therefore turned down, it opens the door for a successful if somewhat lesser request.

For example, assume a philharmonic development staff is trying to raise money for the construction of a new concert hall. Once someone has been identified as a season subscriber to the philharmonic, they may be approached to provide funds on behalf of the construction project. They evidently support the philharmonic, being a regular subscriber, and therefore may feel a commitment to help build the new concert hall. Even so, if they are asked for a great deal of money, say $50,000, they might refuse the request, believing perhaps it is too large an amount for them to provide at that time.

The philharmonic development staff, however, may have asked for $50,000 expecting to be turned down. By refusing their request, the subscriber creates an opportunity for the development staff to ask for and receive a lesser though still considerable amount, perhaps $10,000. The person who turns down a request for $50,000 may jump at the chance to give $10,000 because they feel committed to helping the philharmonic, and are able to satisfy that commitment without paying $50,000 to do it. Turning down the first commitment made it easier to get the second. People who are good at asking for commitments know if they are turned down, it gives them a great chance to ask for something else. This is the second chance dynamic in action.

The Medical Model

A good application of Cialdini's concepts of influence can be seen in the medical profession. An interesting recent development in the medical profession is the movement known as "concierge medicine," which has been adopted by a number of talented doctors nationwide. Using the concierge medicine model, a single doctor only provides service to 200 families, which are each charged a fee of $4,000 a year. In addition to this fee, doctors using the concierge model continue to charge patients' insurance companies for any services they render.

In exchange, the doctor is available to these clients 24 hours a day, seven days a week. Some of these doctors even make house calls. The patients no longer have to wait in a doctor's office, and can call the doctor for any reason, at any time day or night. Should their clients need care beyond their expertise, these doctors will accompany their clients to specialists they have specially chosen for them.

Doctors in the concierge model position themselves as total "health advisors." They serve their patients' health needs in the most convenient way possible for their clients, just as a hotel concierge addresses any and all hotel guests' requests.

The medical concierge model reflects our previously detailed concepts of customer service. Doctors in this model are providing their clients with a level of service they would not expect from anyone else. The doctors have chosen the "right" clients, who are able to pay a substantial fee for this additional service. It is obvious the doctors are good at what they do and have the necessary skills and authority to fulfill their obligations. Clients obviously like their doctors in order to enter into the concierge arrangement. These doctors make a considerable commitment to their patients, and are perceived to be scarce in as much as they will only accept 200 clients at a time.

The medical concierge model holds important lessons for those in the financial advisory business. Many financial advisory clients would be willing to pay a flat fee of $4,000 or more, in addition to other fees and trans-action costs, for superior service from a highly-qualified financial advisor who they like, who works with other clients and families like them, and who will be commit-ted to their financial success.

The future client service model for the financial advi-sory business will most probably look a great deal like the medical concierge model. The most talented finan-cial advisors will provide specialized service to a limited number of clients who need their particular expertise and who will follow their advice.

The Life Advisor

Because they are viewed as knowledgeable and experienced, doctors in the concierge model frequently find their clients asking for information, advice, or refer-rals outside the field of medicine. As they adopt the con-cierge model, financial advisors will also increasingly be asked to provide information or contacts in law, account-ing, medicine, education, and any number of endeavors. Providing this kind of information is increasingly one of the most valuable skills of the financial advisor.

Financial advisors began as customers men who executed trade orders and had few advisory duties. Today's financial advisor has a much greater advisory role, providing guidance on a wide range of products and services. Tomorrow's financial advisor will dispense an even broader spectrum of advice to their clients, espe-cially as the concierge model is adopted. The financial advisor of the future will be a *life advisor* who can coun-sel their clients on just about any subject.

CHAPTER 4

Transitioning to a Life Advisor

How Financial Advisors Can Fulfill Clients' Needs Totally Unrelated to Investing

In the financial service industry, all life advisors are financial advisors, but not all financial advisors are life advisors. A life advisor provides financial guidance, but also advises their clients in almost every area of their lives. A life advisor knows the leading professionals in their community, and can refer their clients to the best legal, medical, educational or any kind of services or resources they require. If a client needs advice to improve their golf game, get their child into college, have a gallstone removed, learn ballroom dancing or prepare a funeral for a loved one, they can turn to their life advisor for information, support and assistance.

A life advisor must have a network of professionals, experts, and contacts to which he can refer his clients.

He must at least know who the best professionals are in a number of specialties, and if possible, have established contact with them in order to facilitate arrangements for their clients. A life advisor wants his clients to be treated especially well by these professionals, and should therefore build relationships with these experts and practitioners. These relationships enable the financial advisor to serve as a life advisor, and also lead to other high-value clients.

If you have sufficiently researched the top professionals in your area, and contacted them, and perhaps created relationships with some of them, you will be in a position to help your clients as a life advisor. Relationships with these top professionals are facilitated by looking for ways to help them at every opportunity, and then using their reciprocal generosity to help your clients.

When a client tells you his father's Alzheimer's disease has progressed to the point where his mother can no longer care for him, you will be able to arrange for the director of the best long-term care facility in your area to take your client and his mother on a private tour of the facility. When you get a phone call from a client who tells you his wife has just been diagnosed with breast cancer, you can get them an appointment with the best oncologist in the area. When a client tells you their son or daughter just got busted with a trunk full of marijuana, you can provide them with the best juvenile defense attorney in town.

When you provide support to people going through crises and are able to help solve the biggest problems they face, when you guide them in all areas of their lives, when you exceed their expectations by orders of magnitude, they will be loyal clients for the rest of your life. This is what it means to be a life advisor.

The Halo Effect

One of the fringe benefits of being involved in the financial service industry is that we become aware of just about everything going on in the world. We do this out of necessity, to stay informed of anything that might influence financial markets, which is pretty much everything, and certainly includes world events, politics, science, business, etc. Financial advisors generally read three or four newspapers and a wide variety of magazines, watch CNBC, CNN, FOX News or Bloomberg, and listen to a number of portfolio strategists, economists, and financial and political analysts on the radio. They read research reports on companies and industries detailing cutting-edge new products and services.

This abundance of information can enable us to become experts on subjects most people don't know much about. This gives people the impression that we are among the smartest people they know, and this in turn provides us with something marketing experts describe as the "halo effect."

The halo effect occurs when people conclude, because we appear more knowledgeable than they are on certain subjects, we must be more knowledgeable on every subject. The halo effect causes people to ask our opinions on a limitless range of topics, many that have nothing to do with financial services. For example, one of our financial services clients might ask us who the best orthopedic surgeon is in the area. Why would they ask us this? It is more or less due to the halo effect. If we are able to provide advice of such breadth and quality that our clients turn to us for answers to the myriad problems they face in their lives, we have an opportunity to become more than financial advisors; we could become life advisors.

Why Become a Life Advisor?

In 1968 and 1969, Richard attended the Wharton School of Finance and Commerce at the University of Pennsylvania, working on his master's degree in finance, and learning a great many new concepts. Wall Street was just beginning to look seriously at modern portfolio theory. It is hard to believe now, but in the late 1960s, time-weighted performance measurement techniques were not used in the financial service industry. More sophisticated performance measurement techniques were not even generally understood in the industry, and were far from being put into practice.

The Wharton School, like many other outstanding business graduate schools at the time, was teaching new performance optimization concepts. Early attempts to study efficient frontiers and optimization models were somewhat primitive in the days before the personal computer, but larger computers at the time could link together to churn out the algorithms and solve the complicated sets of simultaneous equations that helped develop the new performance measurement systems.

In the late 1960s, every class at Wharton seemed to cover optimization models, created to help find the one perfect answer for the optimization of a function under numerous constraints. In the spring term of 1969, Richard had a professor named Douglas Vickers, who forever changed the way he looked at the world. Dr. Vickers postulated people could achieve the "Optimum Optimorum," a tongue-in-cheek expression for the optimum point, by adjusting both sides of a balance sheet until the ultimate optimization was achieved. This fascinating hypothesis stayed with Richard throughout his career, and led him to believe there is always a better solution waiting to be discovered for any situation, including the financial advisor's dilemma: there are not enough high-quality clients to provide for all financial advisors, and not enough time for financial advisors to adequately service the required number of low-quality clients.

Richard found the answer in the financial advisor's choice of clients. To be successful, a financial advisor needs a small number of extremely loyal, high-value clients to whom he provides a range of advisory services. To achieve this, Richard realized financial advisors must be more than financial advisors. What is the Optimum Optimorum client base for a financial advisor? The client base of the life advisor.

A life advisor has a small number of extremely valuable, loyal clients, who receive outstanding customer service, stay with the advisor throughout their lives, and help the advisor acquire other valuable clients. Becoming a life advisor allows the financial advisor to strive for the Optimum Optimorum in their practice.

Richard used this insight to become a life advisor, and after years of remarkable success, decided to share his ideas with other financial advisors, urging those with the talent and acumen to become life advisors. Being a life advisor is enriching in many ways. Richard found that using your experience and knowledge to help guide others to achieve financial and personal success, helping them through the crises in their lives, is not only lucrative, but extremely satisfying, rewarding and meaningful work.

How to Be a Life Advisor

How do you become a life advisor? You start by researching and contacting the 100 most important professionals in your geographic area, and the areas where your clients live. These experts should work in a number of disciplines and industries, including:

Oncology	Long-term care
Juvenile defense	Urology
Internal medicine	Juvenile psychology
Adult psychology	Pediatric medicine
Corporate law	Real estate law
Residential real estate	Commercial real estate
Estate law	Life insurance
Divorce law	Personal injury law
Accounting	Photography
Floristry	Acupuncture
Psychiatry	Neurology
Orthopedic medicine	Radiology
Sports medicine	Cardiovascular surgery
Dermatology	Cosmetic surgery
Architecture	Bail bonding
Jewelry	

In addition, you should know:
Presidents of local banks
Presidents of local universities
Leading guidance counselors

Leading merchants
District Attorneys
The Chief of Police
The Chief of the Fire Department
Leading car dealers
Leading clergymen
Leading contractors
Leading private investigators
Leading security companies
Leading plumbing and heating contractors
Leading electrical firms

You should also know the chairpersons or executive directors of the local affiliates of major charitable and social organizations, such as:
American Red Cross
American Heart Association
American Cancer Society
March of Dimes
National Multiple Sclerosis Society
Alcoholics Anonymous/Narcotics Anonymous
Child and spousal abuse agencies

Not only are the successful people and institutions listed above capable of providing services for you and your clients, they can also lead to potential future accounts.

How do you get to know all these people? How do you get them to be responsive to you and your clients' needs? It isn't easy, but it is certainly possible if you make it a priority.

When you have identified everyone who should be on your list, you should then conduct research to make sure they are reputable, investigating their backgrounds using the library or the Internet.

When you have verified their credentials, you should call each of them and arrange to meet every one. Tell them you are the financial advisor to the most important people in the community, and sooner or later one of your clients is going to need their help, and you want to be in a position to refer your clients to them. Use any resource you can to get to know them. Invite them to breakfast, lunch, or to a business or community event. Ask them about themselves, and see if you share any interests, hobbies or charitable affiliations. Tell them you can't allow another week to go by without making their acquaintance. While this is a considerable task, experience has found that financial advisors focusing on becoming life advisors can reasonably meet and get to know at least 17 of the most important people in their community each year.

Reciprocity can be a powerful force when you need someone's help. When you first meet them, think of something wonderful you can do for them so they will never forget you and will already be obligated to help you.

For example, about 12 years ago, a new luxury hotel opened in Richard's neighborhood. He thought it would be a good idea to have the hotel manager on his top 100 list. He called the manager and told him he was a member of the hotel's spa and tennis club, and that he had a number of important guests and clients coming into town on a regular basis and wanted to make sure they receive the hotel's best attention. Richard invited the manager to have breakfast with him, and they met the following day in the main dining room of the hotel, which had an outstanding reputation and was a favorite restaurant of some very impressive corporate clients.

As they ate their breakfast, Richard noticed that almost the entire staff of the restaurant had passed by their table. He knew they were trying to impress their boss, but they were also checking to see who the boss was having breakfast with. Richard was introduced by the manager to about half of the hotel's staff that morning.

During their breakfast conversation, Richard said how wonderful he thought the hotel was, and how great it was to have such a fantastic amenity in the area. He also mentioned that it was too bad the hotel had one missing ingredient. The manager asked what the missing ingredient was and Richard told him it wasn't all that important. He asked Richard again, and Richard told him it was too bad the hotel didn't have a golf course, as their corporate guests would probably want to have access to a good golf course nearby.

The manager agreed that it was the biggest shortcoming of the hotel, and that all he could do was to send his guests to the local public course, which was sufficient as public courses go, but was not particularly impressive for high-level corporate clients. This was when Richard made his move. Although it seemed spontaneous, Richard had prepared in advance by thinking of something terrific he could do for the hotel manager that would obligate the manager, using reciprocity, to help him in the future.

"You know, I belong to one of the finest golf courses in the area," Richard told him. "If you have some important guests at the hotel, I would be more than happy to have them as my guests at my golf club."

The manager was shocked that Richard would be willing to do this for him. In the next 12 months, he called five times to ask Richard to arrange some golf dates with the hotel's most important guests, who were always either the CEO, Chairman, COO, CFO or other top officer in their company. These VIPs would meet Richard at his club and be his guests for the day. Richard paid their guest fees and provided caddies, lunch, and drinks afterwards. They would often ask to pay for the golf, lunch, caddies or drinks, but Richard always refused to let them. The manager of the hotel also wanted to pay his guests' expenses, but Richard always picked up the bill, which usually amounted to about $300 or $400, a more than worthwhile investment on Richard's part.

The executives would, of course, always ask Richard what he did for a living, to which Richard would reply with his well-honed value statement. Before they left, they almost always asked Richard to call them when he was next in their town and be their guest at their golf club. Richard would go to their town as soon as he could, and would usually play golf with the executive and two or three of the executive's best friends and colleagues, who also asked Richard what he did for a living, to which Richard again responded with his value statement. Through this single initial contact with the hotel manager, Richard met dozens of potential clients. Imagine what happens when you use your list to multiply that by 100.

Life Advisor Relationships

In the previous chapter, we explained the importance of creating a value statement that precisely describes your desired clients, and the skills at which you excel. Only then can life advisors find the right clients who really need and appreciate their services. We also examined the six techniques or characteristics that allow advisors to have greater influence over their clients and can better persuade them to put the advisor's guidance into practice.

Managing and maintaining long-term relationships is also critical to the success of the life advisor. Relationships often fall apart when a client's, friend's or family member's expectations aren't met. Often, their expectations are not being ignored or undervalued, but are merely unclear, unstated or misunderstood. We are frequently asked how to determine our clients' expectations. The answer is very straightforward — ask them. The reason we most often fail to meet clients' expectations is that we don't know what they are because we have never asked. If their expectations go beyond what we can efficiently and consistently deliver, then the expectations must be negotiated, or you must tell the client you cannot meet their expectations and offer to refer them to someone else.

It can be difficult to ask clients what their needs and expectations are, especially when you've been working with them for several years. Life advisors are rightfully concerned the client will be surprised and dismayed the advisor needed to ask them such a fundamental question after working with them for years. There are, however, some diplomatic ways this conversation can be approached.

One way to ask an existing client about their expectations is to arrange a meeting with them and tell them a story about another advisor you know who had his best client leave him for another firm. Explain that the reason the client left was because the advisor didn't do something the client expected, even though the advisor didn't know the client expected it. Tell your client you never want that to happen to the two of you, and suggest you have a conversation to make sure you know exactly what the client expects, which may have changed since you talked about working together several years earlier.

Another way to have the same conversation is to make it part of a regular, periodic meeting with a client. An advisor can tell a client that because the markets change, and clients' situations and needs change, and the advisor's practice also changes, the advisor periodically reviews client expectations to ensure he is providing the services the client needs, in the manner the client expects.

Trust

Trust is essential for successful, long-term business relationships. Trust is gained when life advisors understand, agree to, and meet or exceed their clients' expectations. When advisors have an accurate understanding of their clients' expectations, they must at least meet those expectations, but they also have the opportunity to exceed them. Trust is therefore essential for providing outstanding customer service. You will never learn what you need to know about your clients, and they will never fully follow your advice, without a trusting relationship.

Trust is necessary for turning clients into what Ken Blanchard and Sheldon Bowles refer to as "raving fans" in their book, "Raving Fans: A Revolutionary Approach To Customer Service." Raving fans are those clients who can't wait to tell the world how wonderful you are.

Raving fans are a life advisor's greatest commodity.

Many years ago, Richard worked with a psychologist named J. Mitchell Perry. Dr. Perry was working on the concept of a mutually-exclusive set of principles that would define a trusting relationship. Dr. Perry defined these principles as: **Trust Still, Trust Until, Suspicious Until**, and **Suspicious Still**. Dr. Perry believed these types of relationships were not immutable: people could move from one level of trust to another as our relationship with them developed.

The highest level of trust is *Trust Still*. We usually achieve this level of trust with very few people in our lives. Trust Still is unconditional trust. It means I trust you without question, hesitation or reservation. It does not mean everything you do will always be in my best interest, but it does mean I trust everything you do because you believe it will be in my best interest. This kind of trust is often present in a good marriage, can exist between children and their parents, and can even develop between friends and business partners. Trust Still is worth working for and is to be cherished when achieved. Life advisors ideally like to have this type of relationship with all their clients. The key to reaching a Trust Still relationship with clients is to exceed their expectations every time you interact with them.

The next two levels of trust are the most common. *Trust Until* is just what it sounds like — I will trust you until you fail to meet my expectations. It is a conditional though optimistic level of trust. When someone fails to meet expectations in a Trust Until relationship, they often fall into the next level of trust, *Suspicious Until*. This is also a conditional level of trust, though it is more pessimistic than Trust Until. Suspicious Until is also what it sounds like — I will not trust you until you prove you are worthy of my trust. People usually have to prove they are worthy of trust several times in a Suspicious Until relationship before they move up to the Trust Until level.

In general, most people place others in either the Trust Until or the Suspicious Until category when starting relationships, and will often move people back and forth between these two levels as the relationship gains experience. Often, people will initially place each other in the Trust Until category until one party doesn't perform to the standards and expectations of the other, and are moved to the Suspicious Until level until they earn the other's trust again.

This can occur in the relationship between parents and children. For example, a parent often attends their child's sports activities, and promises they will be at the biggest sporting event of the year, but then for whatever reason fails to show up. When the parent promises to attend the next big event, the child may repeatedly ask if they're going to attend. The child has moved the parent down to the Suspicious Until level. It may take some time before the child restores the parents to Trust Until, and even longer before they elevate them to Trust Still.

The same circumstance exists when children don't live up to a parent's expectations. A child is getting good grades at school, for example, and requests permission to go on an outing with a friend, something the parent normally wouldn't allow them to do. The parent agrees to the child's request in order to reward their good behavior. The parent has reservations, though, and sets clear conditions for the outing, including the time the child is to return home. When the child arrives home much later than was stipulated, and the parent finds out the outing was not what the child described it to be, the child is often placed in the Suspicious Until level until they can again prove themselves worthy of their parents' trust and move back up to the Trust Until level.

The same thing happens between friends. When a friend agrees to meet you at a specific time and place, for example, and then arrives late or doesn't show up at all, you will likely demote them to the Suspicious Until level. Any future plans you make with them, or anyone at the Suspicious Until level, will probably include arrangements that allow you to proceed without them should they fail to arrive.

This also occurs in business relationships. A delivery that does not arrive on time will alter your level of trust in the person who sent it. Often, the person who sent it has made the mistake of promising more than they can deliver. This is one of the most common mistakes business people make. They promise anything and everything to please the client, and then when the work is late or is not what the client expected, trust is diminished and the relationship is damaged. They have been demoted to Suspicious Until, or even worse, Suspicious Still. The client will probably question all future statements and commitments they make. The client may not work with them again, or will waste time monitoring every step of any future projects to ensure its quality and timely delivery.

The well-known business concept of "underpromising and overdelivering" is critical to maintaining trust

relationships. If you give someone reasonable expectations, even if those expectations fall below what they
would have liked, they are more likely to be satisfied
with your work, and more likely to maintain their level
of trust in you. If you exceed those expectations, they
will be pleased and the level of trust will be maintained
or even raised. If you set unreasonable expectations in
an effort to please your clients, however, they may be
happy for the time being, and quite pleased should you
meet those expectations, but you are unnecessarily risking the relationship, as you will lose their trust should
you inevitably fall below the unreasonable expectations
you have set.

As long as people specifically and reasonably define
expectations, they can maintain Trust Until or maybe
even achieve Trust Still relationships. By promising too
much or not defining expectations, you risk disappoint-
ing your clients, falling into Suspicious Until relationships, and even risk losing clients who have lost their
trust in you.

The lowest trust level, Suspicious Still, is the most
difficult to explore because it cannot be dealt with in
a positive manner. Suspicious Still is exactly what it
seems: people who view you as Suspicious Still will not
trust you regardless of what you do. There are those who
think it is the only way to deal with other people, who
see everyone as Suspicious Still, imagining they will
never be let down because their expectations are so low
that nothing can disappoint them. Advisors should avoid
working with these kinds of people, as clients, partners,
coworkers, or in any capacity. They can be infuriat-
ingly suspicious, or even paranoid. They trust no one,

routinely destroy relationships, and always believe other people are trying to hurt them.

Classic examples of Suspicious Still people are the supervisor who constantly monitors and questions employees, or the spouse who continually asks their mate where they have been, what they have done, or how they have spent their money. Working with a Suspicious Still person can be difficult, if not maddening, no matter what kind of relationship you are trying to maintain.

Life advisors strive to create Trust Still relationships with their clients by exceeding their expectations every time they deal with them. Another way to foster Trust Still relationships is by helping clients through difficult situations, which is the Optimum Optimorum of the life advisor's work.

CHAPTER 5

Marketing

Five Ways Financial Advisors can Attract the Right Accounts

The importance of marketing is obvious, but the best marketing approach for a particular business often is not. There are many ways to build a business, and no single way is right for everyone. There are, however, some marketing strategies that have proven particularly successful for financial advisors.

Some marketing methods commonly employed in other industries are not effective for financial advisors. Traditional advertising works superbly for many products and services. If it didn't, smart companies wouldn't spend billions of dollars a year on it. Pharmaceutical companies spend more on advertising than they do on new drug development research.

Print and electronic advertising is seldom a successful marketing strategy for financial advisors. People will take the drugs or eat the food they've seen advertised on television, but when it comes to their money, they won't trust anyone they don't have some kind of personal or social connection to. Maybe giving someone else even a small measure of power over our money is so frightening that we won't trust anyone who hasn't been referred by someone we know, or isn't part of our social or community network.

In the last chapter, we emphasized the importance of targeting the right clients. Financial advisors should use marketing strategies that do just that. There are techniques some financial advisors use to attract large numbers of clients, but the clients frequently turn out to be the wrong kind, costing the advisor more time, energy and sanity than the accounts are worth.

Direct mail, cold calling and seminars can help attract numbers of new clients, but they usually turn out to be the wrong kind. These strategies are effective if you're still reciting the industry mantra, "Open new accounts." If sheer numbers is what you're after, these techniques will work. They will not, however, produce clients that significantly contribute to your income, and will dilute the service you're able to provide to those that do. You're not going to attract many people who have much money to invest. Wealthy people don't go to seminars or respond to cold calling or direct mail. They get advice directly from professionals they know and trust. By using these techniques, you're likely to attract clients that do not generate significant income.

Direct mail, cold calling and seminars are not as effective as they once were for attracting any kind of client. In the mid-60s, few people invested directly in the stock market. Only about 15 percent of households owned stocks or bonds. To encourage more people to invest, brokerage firms provided seminars to help educate potential investors. These seminars were very successful, but their popularity has decreased in recent years as an avalanche of information became available through the Internet and other media.

For many years, direct mail had a response rate of over five percent. Today, direct mail has an average response rate of less than one percent. Charities soliciting long-term donors are happy to get one and a half percent. The success rate is even less than the response rate, as not all responders become customers; many responders are just looking for free information.

Cold calling worked in the past for people selling everything from securities to aluminum siding. When AT&T's monopoly on long-distance service was broken up, the new long-distance telecom companies that arose flooded the phone lines with cold calls, interrupting our dinners and business meetings with endless solicitations. In response, people bought "Caller ID" systems, unlisted their phone numbers, installed electronic barriers to block cold callers, and asked to be put on the company's "Do Not Call" list.

Traditional advertising and marketing strategies never worked well on the most desirable clients anyway, and increasingly don't work on anyone. There are easier and more effective ways to find the right clients.

The value statement, introduced in Chapter 3, should be the foundation of your marketing efforts. The value statement should emphasize your strengths to the clients who can best make use of them. It should communicate your particular skills and target your desired customers. It should convey your value through social proof, authority, likeability, scarcity, commitment and influence.

Once a financial advisor has crafted the perfect value statement, they can use a number of strategies, proven especially effective in the securities industry, to market their business and attract the right clients, including *strategic marketing, niche marketing, community marketing, social prospecting*, and *reciprocity marketing*.

Wealthy families in major cities and regions of the United States have a fairly closed society. They primarily associate with other wealthy families, and they select professionals from within their social group. People of wealth may be affected by mass media when considering a new drug, car, hotel or cruise ship, but not when they're selecting a doctor, lawyer, accountant or financial planner. Wealthy people find financial, legal and medical professionals through personal relationships and referrals, which incorporate the "social proof" described in Chapter 3.

Asking for referrals has been proposed as a natural and easy way to get new clients. Many leading sales managers and marketing experts recommend professionals ask for referrals at every opportunity: from friends, family, clients, people they meet at events, and even people who have refused their cold call solicitations.

This strategy is ineffective because referrals must employ social proof to successfully provide the right kinds of clients. If you ask everyone for referrals, you're casting too wide a net. Doormen do not refer CEOs; they are more likely to refer cab drivers, janitors and receptionists. Professionals should target their marketing efforts at the most desirable clients.

Some sales experts suggest a good time to ask your client for a referral is right after you have spoken to them about a successful product. They recommend you then ask, "Is there someone else you know that you think would also be interested in the same product?" This sounds pretty easy, and it works for a small number of professionals, but it is largely unsuccessful in generating specific referrals for most financial advisors. It is an ineffective strategy, in part, because the issue of referrals does not take place in a focused conversation, and instead is presented as an addendum to another conversation, and is therefore viewed as a "throw away" comment, not taken seriously or thoughtfully by the listener, or the question surprises the listener, who hadn't expected the subject to be raised in an unrelated conversation.

Referrals are a delicate subject and must be handled subtly. Asking someone if you can contact their friends, family, or colleagues can make them uncomfortable and put them in an awkward position. They don't want to refuse the request, but they also don't usually have enough time to think about everyone they know and consider which of them is right for your particular services. When asked for a referral, most people cannot process, in the small amount of time they have to respond, everything they need to consider in order to provide a thoughtful and beneficial response.

The person asking for referrals can often sense the client's surprise and discomfort. In order to avoid hurting their relationship, the person asking for referrals will often quickly change or end the conversation, leaving both parties somewhat unnerved. Hundreds of financial advisors over the years have had similar experiences, and this has led to their reluctance or even aversion to asking for referrals. It is simply not a part of their strategy for building their business. Many advisors have even told us they will only ask for referrals if they are absolutely desperate for business. Even if they are not averse to asking for referrals, few advisors are good at it.

Another successful approach often recommended in the industry is to make referrals an integral part of the client relationship from the beginning. Financial advisors are told they should explain that it is the client's responsibility to refer other potential clients. Some suggest that the advisor should provide a form for their clients to list referral names and contact information so that clients can be allowed to complete the form when it is convenient for them, and when they have enough time to carefully consider which of their contacts is right for the financial advisor's services.

Clients will refer other clients to financial advisors when asked appropriately. If the request is the focus of the conversation, and is made in a way that isn't threatening or demanding, it is more likely to be accepted and acted upon. The key is to do it the right way.

Strategic Networking

One of the most effective marketing approaches we have seen is called *strategic networking*, and is essentially a sophisticated way of getting referrals. Strategic networking suggests financial advisors should focus on their best clients, where they have their best relationships to acquire referrals. It can be a very effective method for developing new business because it plays to the financial advisor's existing strengths and relationships.

Strategic networking is based on an analysis of the top 50 accounts in your existing business. These top clients should represent your target market, the kind of clients you want to attract through your marketing efforts. Your top 50 clients should be the audience addressed in your value statement, and should require the specific skills you can best provide.

Once you have identified your top 50 clients, select the ones that are in a market, profession or business from which you would like to attract more clients. Though you may want to attract clients from all professions, it is useful to slice the market into distinct segments, and then tailor your marketing efforts to each segment. If you have trouble choosing a segment to focus on, start with the one in which you have the greatest number of clients, or in which there are those clients who provide the greatest amount of your income.

When you have chosen a target market segment, collect as much information as possible on the clients in that segment. Where do they live? What organizations do they belong to? What events do they attend? With whom do they do business? Part of this process involves simply asking them, using the four most powerful words in business: "I need your help," or in this case, "I need your advice."

Select the client within your target market segment with whom you have the best relationship. This should be the first person you ask for advice. We recommend you don't ask your clients for help point-blank, but couch your request in an earnest and flattering way, such as, "I am in the process of taking a long-term look at my business. I respect your opinion and I would really appreciate having an opportunity to spend some time with you to get your advice. Is there a good time when I can come to your office to talk with you?" The key word is "advice." In our experience, their answer is almost always "yes."

Once the appointment has been set, you need to prepare for the meeting. It is critical you ask the right questions and approach the meeting with the right perspective. You should have in mind the kind of people you would like to be introduced to: those in your client's particular segment. They might be people in your client's profession, those who belong to the same clubs, live in the same neighborhoods, participate in the same religious organizations, are fellow board members or belong to the same political groups. The list is endless, but varies for each client. Of course, all potential clients still need to be the "right" kind of clients. They should have the money to provide you with significant business, they should need precisely what you are good at and they should listen to your advice.

When you attend the appointment, it is important to avoid discussing the client's account or any business you are doing with them. The conversation should be for the sole purpose of discussing your business. After the appropriate introductory small talk, you should say something like, "I want to build my business for people just like you. I really enjoy dealing with people like you and have decided to focus my entire business in this direction. What are your thoughts?"

Asking the client a general question such as, "What

are your thoughts?" allows them to freely expound on the subject. If you ask a specific question, you will receive only that specific information, but if you ask a general question, you open the door for the client to demonstrate their expertise and provide a wealth of information. Much of what they say may not ultimately prove useful, but you may get surprising responses you could never have anticipated.

As the conversation progresses, you should ask increasingly specific questions, but the phrasing of the questions is important. You want the client to look at the problem from your perspective. You could ask, "Can you give me some ideas about how you would suggest I identify these people?" They may say, "I don't know" and stare at you stone-faced, or they may offer to provide a list of contacts. Be flexible and listen.

Good listening means you have to accept periods of silence in which your clients are formulating responses to your questions. When people are concentrating on a problem, there are often long pauses in their dialogue. Do not start talking as soon as they stop. There is a tendency to get nervous and begin speaking before the client has provided the information you need. This can divert or even end the conversation. Give them time to think. It takes time and effort for clients to remember all their contacts and associations, consider which ones would be right for you, and which contacts they would feel comfortable providing you. Do not distract them with another question or statement when they may be thinking about your problems and issues. Wait for them to completely finish a response, even if it means periods of silence. The old expression "silence is golden" has never been more applicable; their silence might provide you with a golden opportunity.

Ask follow-up questions. Respond to their statements. Be humble and inquisitive. Make it a real conversation, not an interrogation. Ask clarifying questions to be sure you fully understood what they were trying to tell you. Confirm what you think you heard. The longer the conversation continues, the longer they will be thinking about your issues and the greater the opportunity will be for them to come up with additional information.

When you have finished asking them how to best identify other people like them, and have listened to their responses and asked intelligent follow-up questions, you are ready to address the next crucial question, "Would you have some suggestions on the best way for me to contact or get to know these people?" At this stage of the process, help the client find a way to assist you without requiring they make too much effort.

The following are some typical responses:

"Our industry association is meeting in Las Vegas in a couple of months and I will be attending. I always have a hospitality reception in my suite at the event. Become an associate member of the industry group and come to the convention and I will hang out with you and introduce you to some of my friends. It will help you get to know the industry and the people who belong to it."

"Let's set up a game of golf in a couple of weeks at my club. Be my guest and I will invite a couple of other members and will introduce you to them when we're having drinks after we play golf. We can do this every month or so and you will get to know a number of them."

"I am on the board of XYZ Charity. We are having an event in June and I always buy a table. Come as my guest and I will introduce you to some of the other board members and their guests."

"I have a breakfast club once a month with some of my buddies. It is just a friendly, casual meeting. I will bring you as a guest next week."

In general, it is best to gently guide clients into revealing their contacts and providing introductions. There are some situations, however, when the client is not forthcoming, or does not provide specific information or opportunities to meet their contacts. In these cases, you may have to make some suggestions of your own as to how they can help you. You may need to ask, "Are there social events where I could meet people like you?" Or, "Do you belong to any organizations where I could meet other people in your profession?"

In some circumstances, it might even be acceptable to produce a list of people you would like to meet and ask them specifically about these people. You should ask about a maximum of 10 to 15 people on the list. You should do this, however, only with clients with whom you are very comfortable, who won't feel pressured by these specific inquiries.

This strategic networking process has proven to be very successful over the years, even for financial advisors with very different clients and services. One financial advisor's clients were in a specific market segment that only became apparent after he performed an analysis of his top 50 accounts. The advisor had not previously identified this as a niche market. Once he did the analysis, he realized a portion of his top clients could be grouped together into a niche segment. In this case, the segment was a combination of profession and ethnic group. Only after a detailed analysis did the advisor realize he had three clients who were all doctors from the same ethnic group.

We suggested he visit the doctor with whom he had the best relationship. He was initially reluctant to approach the doctor, but then realized it would not be offensive to the client, and became more comfortable initiating a conversation. He made an appointment and had a conversation similar to the ones described above. For the advisor, the meeting was surprisingly comfortable and helpful. The client was very receptive to the idea of focusing on this particular group of ethnic doctors, confirming that they were all financially successful and were mostly interested in equity investing. The client then told him that most members of this group belonged to an ethnic doctors' association, and offered to arrange for him to make a presentation at the group's next meeting. The result was a dramatic increase in business from contacts he made at the group's meeting.

Another financial advisor had a number of his best accounts with people who all worked at the same company. We asked him about doing more business with people at the same company, and realized he had already approached most of the key people at the company, and had secured many of them as clients. He had mortgages with almost all the top executives, managed 401(k) plans and IRA rollover accounts for many of the employees, and handled the CEO's trust and foundation accounts.

He did not think there were any more significant accounts to be gained at the company.

Then we asked him about other companies in the same industry. He told us that most of the other top companies in the industry were located thousands of miles away, and he did not think he could cold call through all the screeners to reach the CEOs, which was how he started his relationship with the current client years ago. During our conversation, however, he mentioned that the CEO had a photograph of a group of people above his desk that he thought were other CEOs in the industry. We suggested this become the basis for his marketing plan.

He called to schedule a meeting with his CEO client. After role-playing the meeting many times, he felt ready. He went to the meeting and opened with the "I want to focus my business on people like you...what are your thoughts?" question. The CEO responded that he thought other people in the industry could certainly use the advisor's help. Then the advisor asked if the photograph over the CEO's desk was a picture of other CEOs in the industry. It was. He asked if the CEO thought these people should be considered. The CEO said he was convinced they could use the same kind of help the advisor had provided him and his company.

The financial advisor then asked how he might be able to get in touch with the other CEOs. His client demurred and said he would think about it. The advisor figured he had gotten close but missed the payday. He was a bit disappointed when he told us about the meeting the next day. A few weeks later, though, the CEO called to invite the advisor and his wife to a dinner, as his guests, hosted by an industry group in New York that was honoring the CEO for his philanthropic work. The CEO even offered to introduce the advisor to some of the other CEOs at the dinner.

When he attended the event, the financial advisor introduced himself to a number of people but was not able to identify who the CEOs were and who were the other guests.

He felt the evening was not going to be as promising as he hoped. What happened at the award ceremony, however, was better than he could have hoped for. When his CEO client got up to accept his award, he said all the usual things about feeling honored to be given such prestigious recognition, but at the end of his speech, he introduced the financial advisor to the entire group and said the advisor had been an integral part of his financial success and the financial success of his top employees, and that he thought other executives in the room could benefit from knowing the advisor.

Astonished and very pleased, the advisor took a bow, and from the contacts made at that event, opened accounts with other CEOs and their companies. These accounts not only generated substantial income, but using the methods of strategic networking described above, led to accounts with other CEOs and companies in related industries. It doesn't always work this well, but every financial advisor can use strategic marketing methods to leverage their top accounts and relationships to increase their business.

Niche Marketing
Niche marketing is used to target a particular audience that shares interests, beliefs, hobbies, or other

characteristics, including a specific social, ethnic or religious group. These niche markets can frequently be approached through an organization, such as a professional affiliation of insurance underwriters or landscape architects, a college or university alumni group, or a hobby organization, such as a classic car club or a dog breeding association. Thousands of these groups can be located through research at libraries or on the Internet.

Any group or association can be used to target a particular audience, even if the financial advisor is unfamiliar with the group's activities, or the organization seems irrelevant to the services provided by the advisor. A financial advisor may know nothing about dog breeding, for example, but if three of their clients belong to a particular dog breeding organization, it affords an opportunity for the advisor to focus on the niche market of dog breeders, and use existing relationships to expand their business.

Activities described in the strategic networking section of this chapter can help identify promising niche markets. Examining your top accounts is a good place to start. Learn as much as you can about your clients. This is one of the most important lessons for a financial advisor. You should know where your clients grew up, where they went to college, what they do on the weekends, their spouse's activities, and their childrens' names, ages, activities and schools. The more you know about your clients, the more effective your marketing efforts will be. If you knew, for example, that three of your best clients had taken cooking classes at a local culinary institute, you could target other professionals and their spouses who take classes at that cooking school.

An analysis of your best clients is the most effective way to mine niche markets because you have an existing advocate, a cheerleader who knows and admires your work and can help promote it. By meeting the people with whom your best clients associate, you also increase your odds of meeting potential clients with the same needs, personality and income as your best existing clients. Remember, the right clients are not just the wealthiest; the right clients are also the ones who need your particular skills, and will follow your advice.

If your best client belongs to a professional organization, consider targeting their industry or profession as a niche market. You may never have thought of dieticians as your best potential clients, but if your best existing client is a dietician, then why not? You certainly never would have thought one day you would be a dues-paying member of the American Dietetic Association, but if your best client belongs to it, you have an opportunity to approach 70,000 other potential great clients.

Ask your client about their professional association, especially its activities and publications. You will often find industry magazines in your client's lobby or office. Ask to borrow the magazines and subscribe to them. This is a simple, inexpensive and effective start to market to people in the industry. Of course, you also have to spend the time to read them and absorb the information. These publications have a wealth of information about the industry and its top executives. You can learn what the top executives think is important, and how to talk to them.

Though an analysis of your best clients is the most effective way to identify promising niche markets, it isn't necessarily the only way. Most financial advisors have had a previous business or professional life before becoming an advisor. They know the language, groups, customs and references in the industry where they once worked. You can use this knowledge and your past affiliations to target niche markets. If you used to be a petroleum engineer, you probably know where they congregate, what groups they belong to, how best to approach them, how to converse with them, and how to gain their trust.

An analysis of your best clients may result in the identification of several opportune niche markets. Prioritizing your activities is essential to an effective marketing campaign; you have to decide which niches to focus on first. Examining prospective organizations can help you choose the right niche markets to target. There are qualities that make some organizations more attractive than others.

Although it is not the only characteristic, the group should be comprised of people who are successful and have money to invest. The organization should have periodic meetings, conventions or other gatherings, and should regularly produce a newsletter or other publication. If a group doesn't have periodic gatherings or publications, it can be much harder to access. The best organizations have established communication and meeting activities.

Once the financial advisor has selected the most promising organization through which to target a niche market, they should try to become a member of that organization. This will provide the advisor and his firm with credibility and access to the association members. A financial advisor should attend the association's conventions and meetings whether they are able to become a member or not, but it is far preferable to attend as a member, an associate member or even as a guest of a member, rather than become a vendor with a table to distribute brochures. A vendor is an outsider; a member is one of the club.

The best way to become a member is to have a client who is recognized and respected within that group. Your job is to be this client's friend and hang out with them at the organization's meetings. If your client is a key member of the organization, he is likely to know other successful people in the group. By accompanying him to events, you will meet other members who will know you as a peer, and may eventually invite you to become a member.

A quick analysis of any association's membership will almost always yield the same results. If there are 10,000 people working in a specific industry, maybe 3,000 will be members of the industry's professional or trade association. Of these 3,000, 300 to 500 may attend the association's meetings. Of these 300 to 500 members, 30 to 50 will represent the majority of the investment capital in the group. These people usually hang out with each other; they are the industry "in" group. If your client is one of them, you can be part of the group by hanging out with your client. Some of these people may hold private cocktail parties at meetings to mix with their peers. This is where you can get the real information about the association, its members, the executive director and their industry contacts.

If you are able to become a member, you should do more than just pay your dues and attend events; you should actively support the association's activities. You should submit articles to the association's publications, provide speakers for its events, enlist new members, and find other ways to benefit the association.

It is important to understand that associations' executive directors are by nature in conflict with their members. The members want valuable services, but don't want to pay high membership fees. The executive director needs services he can provide members for the lowest cost, so he can keep membership fees low and entice more members. This conflict provides an excellent opportunity for a financial advisor to partner with an association, and establish a beneficial relationship with its executive director, by providing valuable services to its members. The executive director will be encouraged to feature and promote the financial advisor's services, and to provide the advisor with even greater exposure to the association's members.

Association publications can help market your services by disseminating articles you have written that demonstrate your expertise. You must submit topical and relevant articles to the association's members, or the publication won't print them. The association is also unlikely to publish an article that appears overtly self-promotional. Avoid personal anecdotes or references to your services. Your business should only be mentioned in a short, biographical paragraph that frequently appears at the end of an article to describe the author. The message will be clear when readers see your name and perhaps your picture on an article that demonstrates your knowledge.

Financial advisors should always check with their firms, however, before they contribute an article to any publication. The firm will want the article to be compliant with its policies. Many compliance departments don't want advisors to write articles. However, the firm may have some existing articles that have been cleared by the compliance department and fit the needs of the association publication. Some firms even allow advisors to claim the "byline" to these stock articles; an advisor can insert his own name as the author when submitting them to the publication. You can also mine your network of clients and prospects as a source of articles, helping your clients as well by publicizing their expertise. The client is happy you helped market their services by getting their article published, and the association is grateful you provided the article.

Executive directors will also be grateful, and may invite you to address the association's members. The executive director has a challenge finding outstanding speakers for their conventions, particularly at the right price. This is another opportunity for you to use your contacts to help the executive director, and use the executive director to help your contacts. Your group of clients probably contains lawyers, accountants, consultants and even comedians who are anxious for exposure and grateful for the opportunity to demonstrate their skills and market their services.

If your firm has a securities analyst who covers the industry you are targeting, they could be a real hit as a speaker. There are also experts outside your firm that might be appropriate, such as an economist, investment strategist or a local professor who studies the industry. They will be grateful to you for the opportunity to speak, and the executive director will be grateful for finding an articulate and informed speaker.

Marketing

You may sometimes be the speaker yourself, but it is preferable to be the person who provides the speaker. You will be recognized for the contribution, and will probably be able to introduce the speaker to the association members. The group will know you helped them, and will realize you have great contacts, reinforcing key elements of Cialdini's theory of influence, discussed in Chapter 3. Among other qualities, providing a prestigious speaker demonstrates your authority and social proof.

One financial advisor we know identified a good client who was also president of his local chapter of the Young Presidents' Organization (YPO). To be a member of a YPO chapter, a person has to be president of a company before they are 40 years old. The members of these organizations are some of the leading young business people in every community. The financial advisor recognized that the YPO chapter would be an excellent opportunity to market his services. The only problem for the financial advisor was that YPO chapters do not for any reason let outsiders into their organization. It looked like it was going to be impossible for the advisor to make inroads into the group until a great idea surfaced that his client, the president of the YPO chapter, thought would be very attractive to the organization.

The financial advisor introduced the YPO group to The Stock Market Game, a fantasy trading program developed by the Securities Industry Association as part of its public education efforts to get more people to understand securities investing. Participants invest a hypothetical $100,000 in a real-time portfolio for a pre-determined period of time. Players can track their portfolios and measure their performance any time during the game. The make-believe orders are placed through the Internet and the accounts are updated daily. YPO members love to compete, so this game was a perfect outlet for their competitive spirit.

The financial advisor worked with a travel agent to provide a great trip for the winner, and an award was presented at a dinner. The advisor provided research and other information to the participants, and the travel agent provided and presented the award. When the contest was over, many of the YPO members opened real stock market accounts with the advisor, significantly increasing his business over the next few years.

Another example of niche marketing arose when we received a call from a financial advisor several months after he had heard our marketing ideas at a formal presentation. At first, the advisor's client book did not appear to contain any good niche opportunities. We asked the financial advisor a great many questions, and learned that one of his hobbies was riding his Harley-Davidson motorcycle. He frequently went on rides with a Harley group comprised of other professionals. The group's members were not Hell's Angels-types, but were more like Malcolm Forbes-type motorcycle riders.

A couple of the financial advisor's fellow riders were already his clients. During a refreshment stop on a weekend ride, he asked one of these clients if they thought others in the group would also be good clients for him. The client thought he should be the financial advisor for other riders in the group, and started a conversation with the other members. The advisor now makes it a point to spend a significant amount of time riding his Harley with the motorcycle group, and has become well known in the group as both a fellow rider and the go-to guy on investing. Riding his motorcycle has become a passionate hobby of his, and a primary source of new business.

We have heard similar experiences from advisors who are surfers, political junkies, ski instructors, bicycle racers, cruise ship fans and stock car enthusiasts. The only limit to niche marketing is the financial advisor's imagination.

Community Marketing

Another great method for marketing your services and building your business is *community marketing,* which can involve everything from donating time to your children's schools, to donating money to a local charity. You may find, through an analysis of your top clients, that some of them are involved in charitable organizations. You should consider being involved in the same organizations as your top clients. Best of all, by contributing to a charitable or community activity, you are building your business in a way that helps others. As the expression goes, you are doing well while doing good.

There are many activities we recommend you pursue as part of a community marketing effort, and just as many we suggest you avoid. Only get involved in organizations that you really care about. Do it because you want to help, not because you want to get business. People involved in charitable or community organizations will know if you try to fake it, and they will be offended by any effort to use their organization solely as a platform to market your services.

Work with leading organizations that are financially stable. There are frankly too many charities trying to do many of the same things. There is no real reason for many of them to exist. Sometimes, organizations are vanity projects, founded by people who just want to be the head of an organization, or to create a legacy by naming the organization after themselves.

Financially-weak organizations should be avoided because they can't provide the services they promise to deliver, their financial insecurity will reflect badly upon you, and being involved with them is simply no fun. The experience can be depressing as the programs often fall short of their goals and fail to help the people they are intended to. An organization's annual report and other public sources of information are easily accessible and will provide all the information you need to determine the financial stability of an organization.

Before getting involved in any organization, make sure the board of directors is comprised of the kind of people you would like to have for clients and associates.

Make sure there are many large donors on the contributors list. If the organization is primarily funded by grants or government subsidies, it may be a great charity but will not provide access to the people you want to meet. Ideally, being involved in a charitable or community organization will afford opportunities to meet people who are the right clients for you. These people will have money to invest, need your services, and will listen to your advice.

Whenever you get involved in a charitable or community organization, make sure your involvement is on the "development" side, contributing to efforts that provide the organization's income, and not on the "programs" side, which delivers the organization's services. There is a rich side and a poor side to every charity. The rich side will provide opportunities to meet wealthy potential clients. The poor side will enable you to work with impoverished or underserved members of the community. While you should believe strongly in an organization's programs, the best use of your time is probably to help raise the money that supports it. Fundraising also usually provides you with a higher level of recognition within the organization, and greater access to top officers and board directors.

To demonstrate your commitment, you need to make a personal contribution to the organization. It should sting your checkbook, but a significant donation will be worth every penny. What constitutes a "significant" contribution depends on the organization. For some organizations, a few hundred dollars might be significant, but others would require a six-figure contribution. Making a token contribution will not demonstrate the commitment needed to gain respect in the organization. Token contributors get token attention. Significant donors sit at the table with the most important and wealthiest people in the organization, and the community at large.

Never get involved in an organization in which the board operates as executive staff. Make sure the organization you are considering has a strong, well-paid professional staff. Without a good staff, the board either has to do the staff work themselves or the organization does not function well and will not meet its goals. Either possibility will prove frustrating for everyone involved in the organization.

There are other staff problems that should be avoided. Stay away from any organization in which the CEO tries to control or micromanage every decision. Also avoid organizations where the CEO serves at the mercy of a dictatorial chairman, founder, primary donor or government organization. In these situations, you will never be able to make a significant impact or provide the leadership that demonstrates your commitment and communicates your worth to the other members of the organization.

There is a very effective way to build your business working with charities without using your own contacts and without spending much time. It may be surprising to many people that it usually only takes five or six phone calls to raise money for a charitable or community organization to be considered a valued participant. A few well-placed calls, handled with care, can secure highly visible contributions that will be greatly appreciated by most organizations. Financial advisors are experts at speaking to people about money who have money, so this should not be too hard to do, especially if you truly believe in the organization's mission, which was mentioned earlier as a suggested prerequisite for working on a charitable campaign.

One way to make a big impact on a charitable organization is to solicit past donors who have stopped contributing. Most charities have a number of people or companies that were significant contributors at one time, but have ceased supporting the organization. They probably have a list of lapsed donors that should be contacted and solicited. Only after a financial advisor has made a significant contribution to a charitable organization should they ask for permission to call these lapsed donors, and for any background information that could help with the calls.

In most cases, there is one of two reasons the contributions stopped: the support was due to a personal relationship with someone who no longer belongs to the organization, or the organization simply stopped asking for the contribution. The most common reason a donor stops supporting an organization is that no one from the organization personally called to ask for more contributions. Many people will not respond at all to mail solicitations. Regular donors are much more likely to respond to a personal call, either because they expect a certain level of personal treatment, or respect, or recognition for their contributions; or because of the subtle social pressure that arise when speaking with a real person.

Donors also stop contributing when their connection to the group was through a personal relationship with someone who is no longer involved in the organization. The member who solicited the original contribution may have moved, had a falling out with the organization, or chosen to focus on other activities. There is also the possibility that an issue arose concerning the organization that dissuaded the donor from continuing their contributions, and no one from the organization offered to provide a sufficient explanation or response to the issue.

Whatever the reason that caused a donor to stop contributing to an organization, the donor probably still cares about the organization's activities, and probably still has the money to make significant contributions, if properly solicited. It is also likely that the donor is wealthy, community-minded, and the kind of person financial advisors want to meet. One way to approach a past donor is to describe an initial telephone call as an inquiry, rather than a solicitation; you are contacting the donor to find out why they stopped giving, so you can address any problems or issues that may be dissuading other donors. Introduce yourself and provide a brief explanation for your involvement with the organization — because you believe in its goals and want to help it grow. Give the past donor an opportunity to talk about themselves, describe their initial support for the organization, and explain why they stopped giving.

Ask questions. This is probably the best advice for anyone approaching another person for any reason, whether it's a romantic date, a business proposition, or a charitable contribution. Most people, including charitable donors, like to talk about themselves, and will appreciate the opportunity to do so. Unfortunately, most people, including solicitors, mistakenly believe the best way to impress someone is to talk about themselves, their achievements and abilities. They couldn't be more wrong. By talking about yourself, you can easily come across as incurious, self-absorbed or boastful. The best way to impress someone, get them to like you, and have them want to do business with you is to ask intelligent questions, and to carefully listen to their response.

Start with the obvious. "I see you used to contribute to the organization. Do you mind if I ask why you stopped contributing?" Once you determine the reason they stopped giving, you can find a solution and approach the donor in a way that will entice them to again provide funds for the organization. By asking intelligent questions in a thoughtful, respectful, and ingratiating manner, you not only increase your chances of receiving donation for the organization, you will also impress the donor, who will want to know more about you.

Soliciting business while calling on behalf of a charitable organization can be construed as a conflict of interest, or worse. Wait for the donor to ask you questions before you launch into the story of your life. You can, however, use a general question posed to you, such as, "How did you become involved in the organization?" to gently steer the conversation to your business. A good response might be, "One of my best clients belongs to the organization. When I heard all the wonderful things the group does for the community, I wanted to get involved and see how I could help." You've mentioned your clients at this point. If they don't follow up with another question, such as, "What business are you in?" then don't push the point.

A personal call or visit to a prospective donor employs many of Cialdini's techniques of influence: reciprocity, social proof, authority, likeability, commitment and scarcity. The donor feels compelled to help you because you are spending your time to call or visit them, which applies the concept of reciprocity. You and the donor care about the same charitable cause, and belong to the same organization, so there is social proof. Financial advisors working with a charitable or community organization have an aptitude with money, and knowledge of the organization and its goals, providing a measure of authority. By approaching the donor with respect, concern, curiosity, and personality, there is a good chance of being liked. Making a significant personal contribution establishes your commitment. The quality of scarcity can be achieved for both you and the donor if your gifts put you both in the small, select status group of contributors. Not everyone can belong to this group, which makes its members scarce.

Remember, you are calling on behalf of the organization, to find out why they stopped giving; you are not making a sales call. A financial advisor can and should tell the donor what they do for a living, if the topic arises, using a concise value statement. The advisor should explain that they always separate their business from their charitable activities. If it seems appropriate, and the donor is the right kind of potential client, the advisor can ask, at the end of the conversation, for permission to call the donor again to discuss other business.

Do not solicit for business when making a call on behalf of the charity. The past donor has an exiting relationship with the organization, its members and perhaps its board of directors. If they feel you are hustling for business when soliciting for a charity, they might be offended and could mention it to someone at the charity. Any business you might attract is not worth risking your reputation. Charity can be discussed in a business call, but business should not be discussed when calling on behalf of a charity.

We worked with a financial advisor who was creating a marketing plan and found he had a strong interest in a local performing arts center. He was a significant contributor, and had been a member of one of the center's support groups for several years. He had acquired a few good accounts through this relationship, but did not feel comfortable actively prospecting for business through the arts center. We discussed community marketing methods with him, and explained that by soliciting contributions from the organization's lapsed donors, he could provide a superb benefit to the arts center, raising money from sources that were no longer considered viable by the group's development staff. He would enhance his reputation with the members of the organization, and get a chance to introduce himself to lapsed members.

Five years ago, the arts center experienced one of those political blood baths that are all too common in charitable organizations. A dispute among members of the board resulted in the dismissal of a very effective and popular CEO, even though the CEO and his contacts had brought in a majority of new contributions. When the CEO left, many of the donors he had brought to the center stopped contributing. These donors represented some of the largest annual contributions to the organization, many in the range of $50,000 to $100,000 a year.

The performing arts center's development staff assumed none of the lapsed donors would be willing to contribute because of the controversy over the former CEO's dismissal. None of these donors, therefore, had been contacted by the organization for five years.

We called the center's current CEO and its development director, and proposed having the financial advisor call some of these lapsed donors to see if he could bring them back. The development staff was very reluctant to participate because they were afraid the donors, many of whom were friends of the former CEO, would be offended by the calls. We wondered how much more offended they could possibly get, considering no one had contacted them for five years after they had invested hundreds of thousands of dollars in the center.

The development staff eventually agreed and the financial advisor made the calls to the lapsed donors. The advisor found, in many cases, the donors were primarily upset no one had called them and no effort was made to understand their perspective or provide a way for them to express their thoughts about the former CEO's treatment. These donors were very wealthy people who were accustomed to being respected and treated well by the organizations they supported. To be ignored after making such large contributions was far more insulting than the CEO's dismissal. Some of them just wanted to be recognized and have their voices heard. Those who were still angry about the former CEO's dismissal at least respected the advisor for making the effort to contact them and hear their side of the story. In the end, the advisor acquired several very good accounts, equally drawn from the lapsed donors who decided to contribute again, and those who were still angry at the organization and did not contribute again, but nevertheless respected the advisor's efforts.

A very effective community marketing approach is to work with your local United Way. When we were branch managers at securities firms, we required new hires to spend two months working as a "loaned executive" at the local United Way. Veteran financial advisors were also invited to participate in the program on a more limited basis. United Way raises a great deal of money through "in-company" payroll deduction campaigns. These programs are popular at many large companies, which believe they gain significant community recognition through successful United Way campaigns. United Way boards of directors are often comprised of top executives from these large companies, as well as other community leaders. A successful United Way campaign is a significant stamp of achievement in a community; it represents a corporate "Good Housekeeping Seal of Approval."

Marketing

The United Way staff, and our loaned executives, work with a company's campaign leaders to manage the "in-company" payroll deduction program. Often, there are promotional enticements for the employees, which can include special prizes, company outings or other fun events. Many financial advisors participating in United Way loaned executives campaigns were placed in companies within the niche market they had already chosen to focus on. They frequently had a chance to meet and work with key executives of the company, which provided very favorable introductions to the entire executive staff.

A sharp financial advisor can make a big impact on the campaign and build personal relationships with key people in the company. Helping to run a successful campaign will also enhance an advisor's reputation among other corporate and community leaders, especially those on the United Way's board of directors. The advisor and their company receive better publicity than they could buy in the media.

Another benefit of participating in a United Way's loaned executive program is the opportunity to meet other loaned executives, which can help build your network of contacts. Some United Ways provide training classes for loaned executives and encourage them to maintain relationships with the other participants in their loaned executive class for years after they participated in a program.

When participating in a United Way loaned executive campaign, you will be introduced to the top management people responsible for the program, who will at some point likely ask you what you do for a living. A financial advisor should have their value statement ready at this point, or anytime they are asked this question. The advisor should emphasize, however, that their goal is to help the company make a successful investment in the community. Only after a successful campaign is completed is it proper for the advisor to ask permission to discuss ways he can professionally help the company and its employees. Never mix business and charity activities. Your objective is help United Way, or whatever charity you're supporting. The relationships you make by doing so, however, will inevitably help your business.

Social Prospecting

Another effective marketing approach, *social prospecting*, takes no extra effort, but it does require some critical thinking and discipline. It's a way to work smarter, not harder.

Social prospecting is exactly what it sounds like: seeking business opportunities through your social life. If handled with discipline and subtlety, social prospecting can create opportunities to meet great prospective clients, and can also help improve the quality of your social life. It does require some critical thinking, a bit of practice, and steadfastly following a few simple rules. On the surface, social prospecting may sound like hucksterism, but if handled professionally, it does not diminish the quality of your social interactions, and can result in additional business. It all depends on how well the concept is executed.

The first and only purpose of attending social events is to mingle and have fun. It is a social event, not a business prospecting event. Don't expect to come out of a social function with dozens of business prospects. If

186

you socialize only to get business, you will miss social opportunities and may push your business too hard and discourage potential clients. Your goal at a social event should be to meet people and perhaps make a new friend or social contact; if they turn out to be a client, that's all the better, but it should not be your primary goal.

The key to successful social prospecting is to avoid directly discussing business while positioning yourself to express your value statement to the right people. When meeting new people, one of the first questions they will you ask is, "What do you do?" Responding with your title and the company you work with will immediately trigger their stereotypical image of a financial advisor. This isn't desirable whether they have a positive or negative image of a financial advisor. A negative image will deter new clients, and a positive image will inevitably result in a typical follow-up question about the market or the stocks you like. A discussion about the markets, the financial services industry or individual investments will solidify the stereotypical image they have of financial advisors, and will likely have nothing to do with your real value to your clients or what you do as a professional advisor. Whether they have a positive or negative image of a financial advisor, it will probably not result in new clients, and won't be a fun or interesting conversation for either of you.

By responding to the polite social question, "What do you do?" with your finely crafted value statement, and can create a flattering image that properly describes what you do. If the person has no interest in your value statement, they're probably not a good fit as a client. If your value statement describes something they need, they will know you are someone who can help them. If this is the case, there will usually be follow-up questions, but don't take the bait. Return the conversation to social topics. You have created the professional image you want; now you must wait to see if there is any real interest by the other party. The best way to answer any follow-up questions is to explain that your business is a bit too complicated to discuss at a party. Tell them if they are interested, you would be willing to call them at another time. If they request your business card, tell them you spend so much time working for your clients and like to enjoy yourself at social events, so you don't ever bring business cards to them. This gives you another chance to employ the "scarcity" concept of influence, suggesting to the listener that your services are so in-demand that you needn't use social events for business purposes. If the person is really interested, they will give you their business card.

Never take business cards to a social event. You can be seen across the room flashing your business card, which acts as a signal to others that you are there to get business, which is not the impression you want to project, and will not attract the right kind of clients. Taking a business card is far less objectionable than giving one. The preferred way to handle a request for a business card is to ask the person to write their name and phone number on a piece of paper, napkin, match cover, scrap of paper, anything. Also get their assistant's name if possible, and ask what time of day would be best to call. All the power is in your hands by having their contact information without providing your own. You control the contact. If you don't want to deal with them, you don't have to call. If you want them for clients, you can pro-actively call them, and get past any screeners by stating the individual has asked you to call.

Social Etiquette

Be professional and courteous at every step, including the way you respond to the invitation. You lay the foundation for your social prospecting from your first interaction with the event. You make a good impression right away by responding to the invitation quickly, whether you can attend or not. Responding "no" is as helpful for planning purposes as responding "yes."

If you responded "yes" and then have to change it to "no," notify the host as soon as you know you won't be able to attend. If you don't, they might print the name tags before you inform them you won't be there, and you will be a glaringly obvious no-show to everyone when they see your name tag lying around during and after the event. An unused name tag left after an event not only notifies the host that you were not there, it also tells them you do not respect the event enough to let them know you wouldn't be coming. Any explanation you later provide will not alter their first impression of you. By calling to cancel after you have already accepted, you implicitly tell the host that you care about their event enough to explain why you cannot join them, and that you have a justifiable reason for not being there.

You can really get off on the wrong foot by responding to your invitation at the last minute. It is the one thing that drives event coordinators nuts. It takes a small effort for you to send a timely response, but can create huge problems for the event coordinator to receive a number of late responses. They might have to call the rental company to change the number of tents, tables, chairs and place settings, and call the catering company to change the number of meals, and call the event location to change parking arrangements or even the room in which the event will be held, which affects signage, audio-visual technical arrangements, and a number of other logistical elements.

Show up on time. People feel there is something embarrassing about being one of the first to arrive at an event. Many people strive to be "fashionably late." There are benefits to being on time, however, even if it means you're one of the first people to arrive. In fact, being the first person to arrive can have distinct advantages.

Unless you expect the party to stop, trumpets to sound, and your attendance to be announced to the entire room, you will join a party in-progress. People will already be engaged in conversation and you will have little understanding of how the event is going except that there is a long line you are about to join at the bar. By arriving on time, you are likely to find the host is not completely prepared for the event, and you will have an opportunity to help them with any finishing touches. You will have private, interrupted time with the host and will have an opportunity to examine the space and get to know the layout.

You could even offer to greet people at the door, if it seems appropriate. You will be helping the host and will have an opportunity to meet everyone who arrives. In a crowded room, meeting most of the people is impossible. By greeting everyone at the door, you will know exactly who you want to spend time with during the event and will already have been introduced; you won't have to break into a group to introduce yourself later. If you need to leave early, you will already have had a chance to meet people, and by examining the space earlier, you will know the most direct and discreet exit.

If your placement at a table is not assigned, never be the first one to sit down at an empty table. If you do, you will spend the rest of your time sitting next to whoever decides to sit next to you. That could be good and it could be very bad. Don't leave this crucial social engagement time to chance. Choose your table companions before you sit down. When you meet someone you want to spend more time with, make arrangements with them to continue your discussion at the table. If you aren't able to make arrangements ahead of time, find someone already seated you would like to sit next to. Make an active choice — don't leave your table placement to random chance.

Thank you notes can make a big impact. Many people don't send them anymore, so the ones you send will really stand out. The event host will appreciate your consideration, and may pay you extra attention at next year's event. If you wanted to speak at one of their events, they are more likely to provide the opportunity.

An excellent example of social prospecting occurred at a recent business awards event. A financial advisor, who had nominated one of the winners, was at the cocktail reception after the event, and there met another finalist he didn't know. When asked what company he was with, the advisor said he worked with people who ran companies to improve their business and win recognition, like the person he had nominated to win the award.

When asked how he did this, he said he had to leave to help the client celebrate their victory, but he could give the person a call if they liked. Having brought no business cards, he was given the person's card and asked to call. Contact was made, a relationship ensued, the advisor got a new client, and the client won an award at the same event the following year because the advisor made sure he was better prepared for it.

Another financial advisor we know met a successful business owner while attending an industry association convention with an existing client who had won a Chamber of Commerce outstanding software firm award. The client was extremely pleased with the advisor because he had presented the client with the opportunity to enter the software firm competition, and had worked with him during the screening process. When the successful business owner asked what he did, the advisor said he made it his business to help clients gain outstanding recognition for their companies, like the client who was standing beside him. The client jumped in and proudly told the whole story of his software firm award, how the advisor had helped him win it, and recommended the business owner get to know the advisor. The business owner became a client and was a winner the following year in a more appropriate and more prestigious recognition program.

Reciprocity Marketing

The final marketing approach we will cover is not focused on a specific industry, company or product. *Reciprocity marketing* can be executed in numerous ways, and is very effective when executed well. Reciprocity marketing is crucial to servicing your most important clients, and is the key to strengthening relationships and getting to know new clients. It is also perhaps the easiest marketing method to put into action. The execution is simple — consistently do nice things for people everyday.

The strongest element of influence, according to Dr. Cialdini, is reciprocity. Reciprocity is essential to being a life advisor, which is based on reciprocal relationships with the people you want to influence. As explained in Chapter 3, doing nice things for people every day is like putting deposits in a bank account of life. Eventually, in surprising ways, the bank account will begin to pay interest on your deposits. Doing nice things for people is easy, doesn't cost much money, takes little time and feels great.

There is an endless list of nice things you can do for people. Reciprocity can be as simple as exhibiting basic politeness and consideration. The most effective reciprocity marketing actions are those that are unexpected. It sometimes only takes a little thought and creativity to make a big impact on your current and future clients.

As we mentioned in the section on social prospecting, confirming attendance early, canceling as soon as possible if plans change, and writing a brief thank you note after the event are several ways you can start a reciprocal relationship. Sometimes, an inexpensive gesture that enhances your client's reputation, like putting a small advertisement in an event program when a client or friend is being honored, can make an enormous impression on a client.

Send letters to people, and a copy to their employers, when you appreciate their excellent customer service. The individual who provided the service and the employer will appreciate your thoughtfulness and professionalism. You might not see a benefit for 20 years, or you may never see a benefit other than the great feeling you have doing something nice for someone. Continually practicing this approach will inevitably have a positive effect on your business and your life.

Sending flowers for small events or recognitions is part of reciprocity marketing. This can have a bigger impact than sending expensive gifts or flowers for major events and awards, where the gesture can get lost among all the others. Sending someone a magazine or other publication on a subject you know they are interested in, or that involves a hobby or interest of theirs, is part of reciprocity marketing. You needn't go out of your way magazine shopping for them; it doesn't matter if just picked up a magazine on an airplane. Knowing that you were thinking about them says a great deal, even if you spent nothing on the gift.

Send cards and flowers for birthdays, anniversaries, or just because you appreciate the people in your life. Your clients are special every day, so recognize them just for being themselves. Sending hand-written notes, according to Professor Charlie Dwyer at the Wharton School, is one of the most powerful things you can do. Do it often.

Consider doing something unique when recognizing events in people's lives. Flowers work, but they are in the trash can a few days later. Los Angeles has an organization that works for a sustainable urban environment including planting trees in the city and the surrounding Santa Monica Mountains. For a $100 contribution, they will plant a small grove of trees to honor births, deaths, weddings or anything you want to recognize. As a living memorial, people frequently visit the trees year after year to see them grow with their children or as a living memorial for a loved one. Tree People sends a framed plaque with the donor and the recognized person that hangs on many office and home walls long after flowers are gone. There are opportunities to do similar things with a local flavor in most communities. Do something unique and special that will last.

Send thank you notes to anyone who has helped you in the past, and express the difference they made in your life. The person you send the note or letter to may have forgotten they helped you and are often surprised and thrilled that it still means so much to you. They are also more likely to help you again if you ever needed it.

There are many things you can do as part of reciprocity marketing that you might only think of doing for a friend, but can make a big impact when you do them for a client. Coaching a sports team for a client's child is reciprocity marketing. So is taking a client's child to work with you to let them see how your business operates. Give clients event tickets you cannot use. Take a client's older child to lunch, give them a practice interview, and counsel them on their careers. Offer to write letters of recommendation for them. When a client's child is interested in working in an industry and you can help them with an interview, introductions and recommendation letters, you will own the client if their child gets the job or not.

Nominate your clients and contacts for professional and business awards. We have experienced first hand the power of this aspect of reciprocity marketing. Anyone who has received an Oscar, Emmy or other entertainment award knows they are in debt to the people who were instrumental in helping them receive the award — you can hear the list of people they thank when they accept it. The same is true for business. Your clients and contacts will be grateful for helping them receive an award. They will be grateful just being nominated, and will look for ways to pay you back whether they win or not.

Ernst & Young sponsors a major, world-class recognition event for entrepreneurs. Other firms run similar programs. These events are prestigious and competitive. There are finalists and winners in several categories. The firms know most of the top people and their companies in each area being recognized, but they can't nominate anyone themselves without the appearance of a conflict of interest, especially if their current clients were to win. They rely on others to nominate people for awards. The nominating process and the ensuing events can provide phenomenal opportunities for financial advisors to generate new contacts and clients.

Most communities have business recognition events. Local business journals, daily newspapers, Chambers of Commerce, ethnic business associations and other organizations provide information on these kinds of events. By nominating someone for an award, whether they are a client or not, the advisor has an opportunity to form a relationship with top officers in the nominee's company, and members of the nominee's family.

One financial advisor we knew made it a practice to become an expert in nominating the best candidates for these awards. To generate a great list of candidates each year, he searched the community for the fastest growing companies, read articles on outstanding individuals, got to know the sponsoring organizations in order to understand their selection criteria, and screened potential nominees. If he didn't know someone he wanted to nominate, he would call them and say how impressed he was with their business, and that he would like to discuss nominating them for a prestigious award. He would also offer to coach the potential nominee, as he had been very successful in helping other people win these awards. He told them it would be more valuable to them than all the advertising they could buy, and that many of the finalist company's clients and suppliers frequently purchase advertisements congratulating them. This advisor became an expert in reciprocity marketing, and his business flourished. He was able to get accounts from over two-thirds of the 20 nominations he has made. These accounts now represent well over $500 million in assets for the advisor.

After a presentation on reciprocity marketing to a group of financial advisors, one of them asked how they could use it in their business. The advisor was a member of a team of three advisors who conducted a half-hour daily radio program on investing. They hoped the radio show would result in a significant increase in their business, but few listeners had become clients. We explained that they were just one more voice in a jungle of stock market broadcasters, there was probably not enough compelling information to entice potential clients to contact them, or they provided such comprehensive information that their audience didn't feel they needed them.

We recommended some alternate content for their

program. There was an Ernst & Young "Entrepreneur of the Year" program in their area. We suggested they use the radio show to interview each of the 30 finalists in the program. This would provide unique local information for the radio listeners and do something very appreciated by the finalists. The financial advisors would be able to meet outstanding company executives on a one-on-one basis.

The nominees gladly agreed to be interviewed, and notified all their employees, suppliers, clients, friends and family so they could listen to the show, which gave the advisors access to an incredible ready-made market. By using their program to highlight these 30 key executives, they were able to open many excellent accounts, and their business more than doubled as a result. They now broadcast interviews with the finalists of every business contest they can find. They found that reciprocity marketing really works when it is well executed.

Smaller events work just as well, as do contests, awards and other recognitions for business people in ethnic groups, for women in business, for the top 40 business people under 40, and other such categories. The list of events can be vast if one takes the time to research them. Your competitors may also be using this strategy. If one of your clients is nominated by a competitor, you will most certainly lose that client no matter how much you have done for them or how good you think your relationship is. Nominating your clients is a defensive move as well as an offensive business practice.

A financial advisor should appreciate any help provided to them, and any nominations given to them, just as they like to be appreciated for their efforts. Reciprocity works both ways, and part of reciprocity marketing is recognizing, appreciating, and returning the favor when someone does something nice for you. Shamefully, not everyone realizes that when someone does something for them, they are in debt to that person and should acknowledge it and eventually try to pay them back in some appropriate manner.

There are some people who only take and do not give back. Don't be surprised if reciprocity only works 70 to 80 percent of the time. The people who do not respond in kind, or at least acknowledge what you have done for them, have sent a powerful signal — they are not the right clients for you. People who do not participate in a reciprocal relationship are likely to be the same "Suspicious Still" people we described in Chapter 4. We recommend you treat them both the same: get them out of your life.

To be a successful life advisor, you must cultivate positive relationships, and discard negative ones. Only by selecting clients who understand reciprocity can a life advisor function effectively, profitably, and maintain emotional well-being and satisfaction. When you deal with Suspicious Still or non-reciprocal people, no amount of effort or generosity will be appreciated, and the relationship will never be satisfying. You will waste your time and energy courting the wrong people. Spend your efforts on people who have the same responsible relationship with the world that you do.

CHAPTER 6

Effective Communication

How to Become a Better Communicator in All Aspects of Your Business

C hapter three explained the importance of providing outstanding customer service, which is at the heart of a financial advisor's practice. Effective communication is also essential to a financial advisor's success. It's an integral component of customer service and all aspects of acquiring, managing and retaining clients.

Too often, financial advisors focus on selling products or acquiring new clients, rather than providing better customer service to their existing high-value clients. This leads to an unsustainable business model, as financial advisors spend their time servicing large numbers of unproductive accounts or acquiring new clients to replace those that have left because they are dissatisfied with the advisor's customer service. This business model will prove increasingly ineffective in the future, as the nature of the business and the changing demographics of American society require financial advisors to compete for a limited number of the same high net-worth clients.

Providing outstanding customer service involves more than the expert handling of your clients' finances. You must of course deliver timely, well-researched and accurate investment advice and achieve sufficient returns on your clients' investments. But keeping a client happy also depends on the way you treat them as a person, the way you recognize their individuality, communicate to them, and service their unique needs.

Financial advisors must learn what their customers need, want and appreciate, beyond big returns. This can only be achieved by listening carefully, processing information effectively, and acting appropriately. Without good communication, the client does not feel they are being served as an individual person, but rather viewed only as a revenue-generating account, leading to an ultimately unsatisfying relationship. Even when financial advisors focus on communications and take courses to improve their skills, poor communication is still the largest obstacle they face to effectively manage their practice.

We have collected a few ideas here that can significantly improve communication in a financial advisor's practice, as well as their personal lives. We know these techniques work, but readily admit we have a difficult time doing them ourselves. Good communication is easy to teach, and preach, but can be tricky to implement in real life. Any efforts to improve communication, however, can have a tremendous impact on your business, and your life in general.

Some people have been called "great communicators" but it's difficult to explain exactly what made them great. Communication is complex, and can involve word choice, ideas, vocal inflection, facial expression, body language, appearance and a host of other factors. An audience can come away from a presentation with a very positive feeling, but frequently cannot correctly recount what was said. They have a warm, fuzzy feeling but have not understood or learned anything. People often focus on peripheral aspects of a speech or presentation, rather the concepts being presented. This is an issue even for great communicators, and can be a serious problem for those of us who have never been accused of being great. The techniques described in this chapter, however, can help anyone, great or not, to be a more effective communicator.

Good communication involves both speaking and listening. A good communicator takes responsibility for both sides of the conversation, whether they are the one speaking or the one being spoken to. You own the responsibility for all communication.

Experts say most people have very short attention spans. Other thoughts come into their minds that can break their concentration, even when they think they are attentively listening. By missing a single key word, a listener can get a very different message than the one intended. Think how often someone begins to answer you before you have finished your sentence. Often, they have little idea what you were actually saying. This is one reason most messages must be constantly repeated, even within the same conversation.

People often interrupt others while they are talking. The primary reason is that we are not really listening because we have something else on our minds that we feel is more important. Sometimes we aren't listening because we are preparing our next statement in our minds, rather than fully absorbing what is being said. Sometimes we simply can't wait to speak because we're self-absorbed, egotistical, or perhaps neurotic.

There are also cultural, professional, gender and generational issues that can hinder communication. We frequently don't have a clue what our kids are saying, for example. Listening to computer nerds talk sounds like they're using some other language. We have to avoid using our own industry jargon so it doesn't confuse or alienate our clients.

The first conversation financial advisors have with their clients is extremely important. It sets the tone for the relationship, and can have a big impact on the client's comfort, and their perception of the advisor's interest in them as a person, rather than just another account. Many times, this first conversation is not effective.

Financial advisors often have developed elegant profile forms for gathering information about their clients that can turn the meeting into an interrogation, rather than a conversation. Standardized forms can provide a consistent client information database, and are necessary for compliance reasons, as they satisfy the NYSE rule 405, "Know your client." However, they may not tell you the truly important things you need to know. Too often, profile questions use industry jargon to satisfy legal compliance requirements, not only turning the interview into an interrogation, but also leaving the client extremely frustrated, because they haven't understood the jargon, and are too embarrassed to ask for an explanation.

Many financial advisors record their clients' responses in small boxes on a form using a range of pre-determined answers: yes, no, above, below, etc. The client interprets the questions' arcane jargon, and the advisor interprets their answers using pre-determined stock responses. The results elicited by the form can end up bearing no relationship to the intended meaning of the advisor's questions or the client's responses. If you want to really communicate with your clients, you must go beyond the form, you must think outside the boxes. Clients are human beings with complex egos and emotions that aren't addressed on a standardized form. There is no box for how a client feels.

All great communicators use stories, examples or parables to get their message across. It is more effective to demonstrate a concept than to describe it. To emphasize an important concept, good communicators frequently abandon descriptive language; they use quotes, analogies and anecdotes. This technique can very effectively communicate even the most complex idea to a varied group of people. However, you must choose your examples wisely. A story that does not accurately depict the idea you are trying to present can be just as damaging as not using one at all, or even more damaging if it confuses the audience. Avoid stories that contain abstruse or idiomatic language, or cultural, industry or professional references. Analogies can confuse or distract an audience if the relationship between your ideas and the analogy is not crystal clear.

Quotes, which are often lifted from books of quotations, sound nice but can lead people in unintended directions. Make sure the quote reflects the intended message, and doesn't contain any distracting elements. Humor can be used to enhance communication or to relax the audience and break any tension in the room; but again, make sure any jokes you tell don't detract or distract from your message, or offend anyone in the room, or anyone outside of it. We have all heard politicians make jokes that are warmly appreciated by the particular group of people they are addressing at the time, but which create enormous controversy and problems for them when reported on the evening news. Try to imagine if anyone would be offended by a particular joke: your grandmother, your daughter, your golf buddy, a conservative minister or a liberal professor. The way information travels on the Internet, a harmless joke could create a public relations nightmare. If it could offend anyone, better to leave the joke out of your conversation.

Listening

One of the most important techniques to master is the art of listening. Listening seems easy enough; we do it throughout the day without making much effort. Truly listening to someone, however, takes a great deal of effort and is anything but easy. Listening requires as much concentration as talking, or more, in order to absorb a stream of conversation, process and sift it, store important new information, and take mental notes to respond or react to the conversation. Listening is an active skill.

Effective Communication

We rarely listen effectively when we're on the phone. Think about what you do or have seen other people do while talking on the phone. While supposedly listening to the person at the other end, we will watch television, read a magazine, send e-mails, review documents, or observe other people in the room who are talking or writing on a flip chart. We will even converse with other people in the room, by whispering, covering the receiver with our hand, or muting our phone. We rarely focus entirely on what someone is saying.

We don't even listen when we're talking to someone in person. You have probably been in a situation at a social party in which you are talking to someone you were just introduced to whose name you have already forgotten. Obviously, you were thinking about something other than their name. At the end of the conversation, you can either say goodbye without using their name, or you can ask them their name again. If you say goodbye without using their name, you have lost an opportunity to ingratiate yourself. Remember, one of the keys to influence is likeability. Everyone likes being addressed by his or her name. Using someone's name establishes a friendly familiarity between you; it's an easy way to get someone to like you and feel comfortable with you. If you ask the person to repeat their name, it's a sure indication that you either weren't listening to them, or felt the information wasn't particularly important. Either way, not remembering someone's name is indicative of poor listening skills.

Continuing with the party scenario, imagine you are talking with a group of people, and someone other than you is telling a story. After a short time listening to the story, you come to the conclusion that you have a much better story to tell. When the person telling the story takes a breath, you break in and tell your more interesting story. You may believe you are saving the group from having to listen to the other person's boring story, but no matter how interesting your story is, you have sent a clear message to everyone in the group that you think the story you interrupted is boring or worthless.

Some people don't even wait for someone telling a story to take a breath; they interrupt people by talking over them or talking louder than them. Sometimes they are simply impatient, or perhaps they confuse self-confidence with self-importance. In any case, they are not going to be likable to those around them, will not attract quality clients, and won't be able to effectively service the clients they have.

Some people even finish other people's sentences, not only interrupting them, but also presuming to know what they're going to say. This is a clear indication that they are not really listening to what the other person is saying. Some people are so rude as to finish other's sentences out loud, while most of us to some extent finish people's sentences in our minds, which may be less rude, but still indicates a failure to listen effectively. By finishing other people's sentences in our minds, we are likely not to hear or understand what they are really saying.

The Three Second Rule

One technique to aid effective listening is to employ the "three second rule," which dictates the listener wait three seconds when someone pauses in their dialogue before responding. Count to three slowly: one thousand one, one thousand two, one thousand three. It's a long time in the context of a conversation. The three second rule ensures you won't interrupt someone in the middle of a story, or the middle of a sentence, if they are pausing to take a breath. It also gives you time to absorb what the person has told you, and craft a concise, thoughtful response, or at least appear as if you are doing so. In any case, the three second rule indicates to the speaker that you were listening and processing what they said, and that you respect them and value their ideas. These are essential ingredients in the client-advisor relationship. Clients and advisors should like, appreciate, respect and value each other. It would be odd to constantly tell someone, "I really like and appreciate you, and I respect and value your ideas," but the three second rule does just that, in a way that is polite, thoughtful and will always be appreciated.

The three second rule must be applied judiciously, however, and tailored to the particular conversation. It's more of a tool to use when needed than an ironclad rule. If you are at a social gathering, the likelihood that you won't break the three second rule during the whole evening is near zero. In addition, there are settings in which abiding by the three second rule is impractical, and would result in your never saying anything the entire evening, which can make people think you are ill, or just a bore. It works especially well, though, during a one-on-one conversation with a potential or existing client.

Effective listening also involves processing information, and making accurate judgments about existing or potential clients. Problems arise, however, when we try to neatly fit people into categories, when we treat them as types instead of individuals. People are not only unique, they are also complex, paradoxical, and at times, self-contradictory. A good example of fitting people into existing categories can be seen in some of the matrix questions used to define clients' risk tolerance.

It is essential for a financial advisor to ascertain the amount of risk each client can tolerate in order to recommend the right products. Some advisors use standard sets of questions to determine risk tolerance. The questions are widely available and circulated within the industry. One questionnaire asks how the client feels about bungee jumping. Apparently, someone concluded that the perceived risk of bungee jumping had some correlation to investment risk tolerance. It does perhaps, for some clients. It is also possible that a person afraid of heights would be comfortable with the investment risk profile of a Mississippi riverboat gambler.

In too many cases, financial advisors don't give their clients a chance to tell them what is really important to them. Many years ago, we knew a three-man team of institutional brokers who jointly provided services to bank trust departments. Each week, two or more of the team would talk to the investment officer at each of their client banks. One of them always had the lead client relationship responsibility for each account, but another team member would also talk to the client. They would then have a weekly work session to compare notes on each account.

Unfortunately, the broker who had the lead relationship with their largest accounts had very poor listening skills. He had the particular problem of never allowing one second of silence in any conversation. If anyone with whom he was speaking stopped talking for even a second, the broker immediately jumped in to say something. Another partner with much better communication skills had a conversation with the Chief Investment Officer (CIO) of a bank that was one of their biggest clients. The CIO suggested he could never really tell the lead broker what he needed because the two of them had very different communication styles. The CIO spoke very deliberately and slowly, and often paused to collect his thoughts in order to be absolutely precise, while the broker, as we mentioned, leapt in to fill every pause. Consequently, the CIO could never finish a thought, and could not accurately communicate his bank's needs.

The partners had a candid conversation in which they discussed the broker's communication style. The lead broker agreed to visit the CIO, specifically ask what the bank needed and wanted, and then not say anything until after the CIO had spoken and left a pause of silence for at least 30 seconds. The broker did just that. He asked the client, "What would you like me to do for you?" and then he shut up, keeping one eye on the second hand of a clock on the CIO's desk. The CIO sat in silence at his desk, looking at his hands folded in his lap for over 20 seconds. Then he lifted his head to face the broker and slowly said, "I wondered if you would ever shut up long enough for me to tell you the three major things I need from you."

For the next 45 minutes, the broker did not say a word, even through several long silences. At the end of the 45 minutes, the CIO smiled and said, "Thank you for listening to me. I really need your help." That meeting created the foundation for several major projects that doubled the group's income from that particular client. The lead broker applied the communication lessons he had learned to his other accounts, and the group prospered.

Confirmation

Financial advisors often use financial jargon that is not understood or is misinterpreted by their clients. This can be avoided, and communication in general dramatically enhanced, by using the technique of confirmation, which is when you confirm what you have said by having the listener repeat it back to you. Confirmation is especially essential when you are saying something important that you want your clients to understand and retain. You should say something like, "I don't always communicate as well as I would like and it is very important that I know you understand what I just told you. So just to be sure, tell me what you understood me to say." When you employ this technique, you will be in for the biggest surprise of your life. People will respond by telling you something that, in your mind, bears no relation to what you just said. You will wonder if the two of you were in the same conversation.

Communication is often like the 1950s television program that became a party game called "telephone." In the TV program, 12 people sat in chairs in a row. The host would whisper a short phrase in the ear of one of the people at the end of the row, and they in turn would whisper to the person next to them, who whispered it to the next, until the last person to get the phrase would stand and say what they heard. The results were fascinating, and indicated a great deal about the way people think and communicate. Very seldom did the last person's statement even remotely resemble the phrase that was uttered to the first person. Even well known phrases and clichés were garbled as they passed through the telephone chain. Oddly, nursery rhymes came out the other end as different nursery rhymes.

Something like the telephone game probably happens to you every day. You thought you'd made yourself perfectly clear, only to find the person you were speaking to came away with something completely different. Several years ago, a "take no prisoners-suffer no fools" CEO of one of the largest securities firms in the nation told a group of his firm's analysts that he wanted to see how the different market indexes had performed compared to one another over the past several years. Orders in hand, everyone left the room.

A couple of months later, the CEO called in the head analyst and demanded to know where his information was. The head analyst told the CEO that two of the other analysts he had spoken to had been working non-stop on the project and would have it completed within the week. The CEO shouted, "You have been doing what? I asked you for one of those Ibbotson wall charts!" The CEO couldn't believe that some of the supposedly smartest analysts in the industry wouldn't immediately know what he wanted. The analysts couldn't believe their CEO wouldn't ask for an Ibbotson chart by name. They thought he wanted an original comparative analysis of markets going back several years. Had he asked for confirmation to ensure they understood exactly what he wanted, he would have had his wall chart, framed, likely before the end of the day.

Confirmation works both ways, whether you are

the speaker or the listener. When you tell someone something, confirm they heard what you meant. When someone tells you something, confirm you heard what they meant. Repeat it back to them so you know you got it right. You could say something like, "What you have just said is very important to me. I want to make sure what I heard is what you said. Let me tell you what I understood you to say." Repeat what you heard in your own words. You will probably be close, but in more cases than not, they will make some clarifying adjustments. In the previous story about the senior analyst and CEO, the CEO could have solved the problem by confirming what the senior analyst heard, but the senior analyst could have also solved the problem by confirming what the CEO said.

Confirmation is particularly important when giving someone instructions you want them to follow, whether they're a subordinate or a client. People are reluctant to admit they didn't understand instructions for fear of looking unintelligent. They may not tell you they didn't understand your directives. They might think they can figure it out later or ask someone else. They might ask someone who has no idea what you wanted, and that person may know they have no idea what you wanted, but having been asked, they are reluctant to plead ignorance, and may provide faulty information. When you ask someone for something you really need, confirm they know what you want and how to do it.

Broad Client Profiling

It is impossible to effectively profile your clients using only formal interviews or financial questionnaires administered in your office. These tools provide an incomplete picture. To be a successful financial advisor, you should know as much as possible about your clients. You should profile the whole person, not just their assets, and not just the face they present in your office. Learning as much as you can about your clients, and treating them as unique individuals, will enable you to better serve them.

To learn as much as you can about a client, you should visit them in their home and office. Seeing someone's home or office is one of the most effective ways to gather information about them. There is a core to each person, but there are also roles we play in different settings, faces we show the world depending on where we are, what we want, and to whom we are speaking. To understand the whole person, you must see as many of their faces as you can.

An excellent way to get a sense of the individual client is to see them in different environments. When you visit clients in their homes or offices, there will be clues all around you that reveal elements of their personality. Clients' offices are a treasure trove of information for financial advisors. From the time you enter the door, you can begin to pick up clues. Decorations tell their own stories. How the office is maintained says something about the client's attention to detail and image. Plaques and trophies can tell you what they value. What is not in an office can also be quite revealing. A series of Little League baseball trophies, for example, indicates the client may have participated in Little League, or perhaps their son or daughter does, or they value children's sports, or appreciate baseball. In any case, it reveals they have an interest in Little League, and that information can be used to better relate to them, serve them, and obtain additional clients.

The dress, formality and professionalism of the client's assistant or support staff can tell you how they deal with the public. You can better observe the behavior of the client's executive assistant if you sit near them while waiting to be admitted to your client's office. Any interaction the assistant has with you or the public should be noted. Many executives have their assistants profile visitors, so be careful what you say to them. Try to cultivate a respectful, professional and personal relationship with this "gate keeper."

An individual's office is a wealth of information. Many people have an "I love me" wall with pictures, plaques and recognition certificates that can tell you a great deal about them. If the person has a large United Way recognition plaque on their wall, you can use this information in many useful ways. For example, if you are a recognized contributor to the United Way, you have a common interest with your client, and it probably wouldn't hurt to wear your United Way pin the next time you see them.

What people choose to put on their office walls says a lot about who they are. A picture of a golf hole, for example, normally has a story behind it that is very important to the client, and provides an opportunity to learn more about them. "There must be quite a story behind this picture," you might say. You could even follow-up on the conversation by sending an interesting article about a new golf course, golf club, or some other golf-related item. In this way, you can use information

216

gleaned from their office to do something unexpected the client will appreciate, enhancing their customer service experience with little effort or expense on your part.

Any picture can be the starting point for a conversation and an opportunity to learn more about your client. Personal photographs can be used to help bond with the client. Pictures of a spouse, kids in soccer uniforms, or a baby in a cradle, for example, can provide opportunities to enhance your personal relationship with the client. A lack of pictures, plaques, or trophies tells another story: this is most likely a "strictly business" client who may not have a great appreciation for personal conversation. Use what you see. If you see a photograph of young kids wearing soccer uniforms, you should bring it into the conversation with a statement like, "Looks like you have several years of soccer in front of you."

If you see a plaque thanking the client for their support of a particular charity, consider making an unsolicited donation to that charity. This can cement a relationship much more effectively than a lunch meeting or a golf game. Send an informal note to the client that says something like, "I just wanted to thank you for your continuing support. I have sent a check for $100 to your favorite charity." Or you could send a contribution to commemorate an event in your client's life, in which case the informal note would read something like, "Congratulations on the birth of your child. I have had the Arboretum Society plant a grove of trees in honor of the event." This type of gesture can really impress a client; it lets them know you are thinking about them and care about them as an individual.

Rod was a branch manager in the Pacific Northwest

for several years. He had an "I love me" wall full of awards and recognition plaques, as well as a number of photographs and other personal items around his office. Peter von Reichbauer, his state senator at the time, came to Rod's office one day for a visit. His executive assistant took the senator into Rod's office and spoke with him for a few minutes before their meeting. By the time Rod entered, Senator von Reichbauer had acquired a wealth of knowledge about him by examining the items in his office. The senator had been in his office for less than five minutes, but in that short time, he had developed an uncanny, in-depth understanding of Rod's life. He read the walls of Rod's office as if he had been reading a book on Rod. Senator von Reichbauer touched on subjects that were important to Rod and quickly established a strong personal relationship. The senator employed this technique to great success throughout his career; people liked him because he seemed to be so interested in and focused on things that were important to them.

The same techniques can be applied when visiting someone in their home. These visits are likely to tell a financial advisor far more about a client, especially about their family, background and hobbies, than any conversation or questionnaire administered in an office. When you visit someone in his or her home, it changes the dynamic of your relationship, allowing you to establish a connection that turns even a formal business arrangement into a personal relationship. You also implicitly convey that you see them as an individual, and not just as a revenue-generating account. In addition, you have the opportunity to ingratiate yourself not only to the client, but their family as well.

Formal interviews are greatly enhanced by information gathered informally. Even when administering a questionnaire, you should take the time to ask the client about their outside interests or hobbies. Be sure you record their answers as accurately and thoroughly as possible. Formal and informal conversations elicit different responses, and provide different information. Formal interviews focus on facts, while informal conversations focus on the person. They can both be used to further your understanding of the client, and improve your ability to serve them.

Modeling
Profiling a client during an initial meeting can be difficult. People you don't know don't usually volunteer a great deal of essential information. You want to build a comfortable relationship, but you also need to acquire necessary details about your clients. If you use an interrogatory style, it will be hard to build a comfortable relationship. Nobody likes being interrogated. If you spend all your time building an amicable relationship, it will be harder to get the necessary information. One way to stay conversational while still learning what you need to know about a client is to use the modeling technique.

The modeling technique is based on the tendency to model other people's behavior. If you want someone to open up to you, open up to them first. New clients want to know about you as much as you want to know about them. They may have seen your bio, brochure, or list of services, but they can only assess your suitability by meeting you in person, just as you are assessing their suitability. The modeling technique satisfies their need to know more about you, and opens the door for you to know more about them.

Using the modeling technique, a financial advisor would say something like this to a new client, "I would like to get to know you better, so let me tell you something about myself and then you can tell me about yourself." The advisor then proceeds to tell the client about themselves, but in a very deliberate, directed way; it is not a random monologue about yourself, but a well-planned speech that mirrors what you want to know about your client.

Make a list of the things you want to know about the client. Remember, you want to know about the whole person, not just their assets. You want to know where they were born, where they have lived, what schools they went to, what degrees they have earned, what jobs they have held, their marital status, their children and grandchildren, the mortgage on their house, their hobbies and interests, any charitable or community groups they belong to, and anything else you think would be useful.

Respond to each of items on the list, providing information about yourself: where you were born, where you have lived, etc. This forms the basis for your opening explication. It might go something like this: "I grew up in Indianapolis, Indiana, and got a degree in engineering from Purdue University in 1968. I worked for General Motors for several years in Detroit before deciding my future was really in the financial services industry. I went to work for Shearson and Company, which has been bought and merged several times. I met my wife in college, and we were married in 1970. We have three children — a daughter, 30, with two grandchildren; a son, 27, still looking for the right girl; and a daughter, 23, starting a Ph.D. program at Duke University. I still have a mortgage on our third house. I like international travel, as long is I can play golf along the way. Tell me something about yourself."

By providing specific personal details about yourself, the client is apt to feel comfortable revealing the same information. They will likely tell you the same things about themselves that you have told them about you. If they leave out any important details, you can always follow up with another question. The whole conversation usually takes less than 10 minutes.

If you don't believe modeling works, try it the next time you are in a group of people introducing themselves. If the first person says three things about themselves, everyone else will usually reveal the same three things. If the first person mentions where they work, the number of children they have, and the sports they like watching, you'll likely observe the rest of the group providing the same information.

We have demonstrated modeling in many presentations we have given using someone randomly selected from the audience. We tell the audience member three things about ourselves, and then ask them to tell us about themselves, and see if they will reveal the same three items. We are always fearful we will choose one of the 10 percent of people who won't reveal personal details, but we have never had this happen and the experiment has always succeeded. In many cases, people observing in the audience tell us they have known the person for years and never knew some of the things the person revealed in public to a group of strangers. That is the power of modeling.

Saying What is Important

We say a great number of things to our clients. Frankly, most of what we say is unimportant, if not meaningless. Once in a while, we have something truly important to say to our clients. If we don't somehow indicate its importance, the information is likely to be overlooked by the client, or lost amongst all the unimportant things we are saying. There are several ways to draw attention to important information you are conferring to your client. When you are going to say something important, tell them it is vital they understand what you are about to tell them.

When you are saying something important, say it differently. You should always start with a pause, in order to separate the forthcoming information from the rest of the rubble you have been saying. Then, when you say something important, say it slowly, speaking distinctly and forcefully. To make sure they understood what you wanted them to, get confirmation by asking the client to repeat the information back to you. Better yet, only say important things. Then you'll never have to worry about distinguishing the important from the unimportant.

An even more emphatic way of drawing attention to important information is to tell the client to write it down. People understand and remember a concept much more thoroughly when they write it down themselves. They will also be able to repeat to you exactly what they understood you to mean, and will have a record of the information. It may seem awkward to ask a client to write something down, but there are ways to make both of you feel more comfortable about it.

You should say something like, "This is very important, so humor me. Get a piece of paper and write down the following." Or, "It can be difficult to accurately convey information in a verbal conversation, so please get a piece of paper and write this down." Or, "I never seem to make myself correctly understood when I verbally describe this concept, so please get a piece of paper and I will walk you through it." This works particularly well when explaining something to a client while on the phone.

Communicating with Seniors

People are living longer, the general population is aging, and wealthy people are getting wealthier the longer they live. The best clients are therefore often the oldest clients. People need financial and life advice well into their 80s and 90s. Their children will often be retired before their parents die. To help elderly people with their estate planning, you will have to know how to communicate with them. It is therefore essential for financial advisors to learn how to talk to senior citizens.

In our rush to move on to the next client, the next meeting, or the next event in our lives, we frequently miss an opportunity to effectively communicate with older clients. We tend to have a set communication style we use with all our clients, but effectively communicating with older clients can require a much different style of communication that the one used with younger clients. The difference is often not so much in what we are saying, but in the way we are listening.

Don't treat older clients like children, or as if they're unintelligent. Don't necessarily speak loudly or slowly because you assume they all have hearing problems. Don't assume all older clients need or want the same things. Senior citizens are individuals with unique concerns and needs, just as younger ones are. Many do have hearing problems, however, so make sure they are correctly hearing you. People with hearing difficulties get tired of saying "what" when the volume is too low, or when someone is speaking too quickly or not clearly enough. People frequently don't indicate they're having trouble hearing you, though they can often figure out what you are generally saying, even if they don't hear every syllable. You should make a special effort to confirm everything you are saying when speaking with an older client. Again, you own responsibility for all communication.

Older people often have a different communication style than younger people. Don't expect older clients to provide concise nuggets of information. You may think they are wandering in their conversation and losing track of what they should be telling you. They may take what appears to you to be a circuitous route in order to get to the information you require. You must understand that older clients have a lifetime of experience and can see connections between ideas that you may not. They may sound as if they are conveying a story that is unrelated to your question, but many times, it is the story that you really need to know. If you are patient and listen carefully, you will likely find their story provides a meaningful context for the answer to your question. Older people see the whole picture of their lives, and every connection between the disparate parts. A story about their grandchild's swim meet might remind them of a summer they spent in Arizona. Follow these stories, and you will find golden nuggets of information along the way.

David Solie, CEO of Second Opinion in Woodland

Hills, California, has probably done the best work we have seen to help financial industry professionals communicate with older clients. David is one of the top consultants in the country dealing with the implementation of large estate planning programs. His newly-published book, "How To Say It to Seniors, Closing the Communication Gap with Our Elders," is one of the most important resources to help advisors deal with seniors.

In an article in the February 2001 issue of Senior Market Advisor, David Solie is quoted as saying, "Whether they're patients of physicians or clients of lawyers, a senior's behavior is frustrating at times. I'll give an example: Older people tend to speak and conduct their conversations in a very nonlinear fashion. Younger people, on the other hand, are very sequence-driven. We pride ourselves on that; we consider that a mark of organization and accomplishment. When seniors start to wander in nonlinear conversation, we become angry with them and we try to get them back on task, because we assume that nonlinear conversation is a sign of aging and failing organizational skills. The truth is that nonlinear conversations serve a huge function. The nonlinear connection is not necessarily random, not necessarily confusing. Quite to the contrary, if you pay attention to the nonlinear, the discoveries can be overwhelming."

When asked what a financial advisor has to gain from following the nonlinear conversation of older people, David responds, "I think they get two big payoffs. One would be the financial; another would be the ability to come up with access to and work with the real needs of the client. I always tell people that a person's legacy will never be self-evident. You're going to get real creative at helping to extract the legacy. Older people have a lot to teach us, even though we're so absolutely sure that we can't be taught much of anything. They really have some wonderful things to teach us."

Older people often have more time for conversations. They are making possibly the last and most important decisions of their lives, decisions that will define their legacies. They may want to say it in a very rich, full and meaningful manner. By listening to an older client's nonlinear conversation, financial advisors can learn about a client's life, their desires, and other important information they can use to better serve their clients.

As often as not, older clients avoid estate planning, either because they don't want to think about or discuss their death, or because they haven't determined their true legacy. Many times, their children assume they are their parents' legacy and want the estate plan properly drawn to ensure they get all the money. If the children are not the only legacy, seniors may very much need you to help elicit their true desires.

Advisors, attorneys and consultants working with older people frequently focus on the wrong issues. Most of these professionals believe that estate planning is a function of getting the most money to the children and grandchildren by paying the least amount of estate tax. That is indeed the case in many families, but this singular focus can be very disconcerting to older people. In many cases, they have already done a great deal for their children and grandchildren and may feel there is more to their legacy than their family.

As people grow older, they think about the meaning of their lives, and what they will leave behind in addition to their offspring. They search for their legacy. Many times, this search is only an undefined longing. Older people may know there is more to their legacy than their children, but they may have never clearly defined what it is. You may have to help them find their legacy. There may be major events or experiences in your clients' lives that their children either don't know about or have dismissed as uninteresting or unimportant. It is up to the financial advisor to draw out these events. Listening to their older clients' nonlinear stories, as David Solie recommends, can help advisors understand their clients' lives, and help their clients determine their legacies.

Advisors can have a very gratifying experience helping clients discover their legacies. Most people have not identified an institution, charity, or other cause they want to support after they are gone. The institution may provide a naming opportunity to perpetuate their legacy, or the client might be solely motivated by a desire to help other people.

David Solie suggests advisors take the time to listen to everything their older clients are saying in order to establish a relationship in which a conversation about their legacy can comfortably and effectively take place. Listen carefully to even what may seem like a rambling conversation that strays far from the original subject. These divergent discourses are rich with details that reveal much about the client and could suggest possible legacy institutions or causes.

Don't expect immediate action once you help older clients identify their legacy. Older clients may hesitate to implement the estate plan you have helped them develop. You may both agree it is an excellent plan, yet they might not be ready to act. Many times, it is because they do not want to give up control over their lives or their assets. Selling a home and moving into an assisted-living facility changes their perception of their control over their lives, even if they know it is in their best interest. If this is the case, an advisor should back off and avoid pressuring the client. Let them know they are still in control of their life and their estate, and any decision is theirs alone. They may take a long time to make a decision, or they may not ever decide to relinquish control, but it must be their decision. If you pressure a client, they are certain not to relinquish control.

Older people frequently represent a large part of your business as a financial advisor. They will increasingly need your help the older they get. You will provide some of the most important advice they receive at their age. In order to give the best possible advice, financial advisors must be extraordinary listeners. It can take time, but it is a great investment.

Conclusion

Superb communication skills are essential for financial advisors to successfully serve their clients. It is crucial for advisors to learn as much as they can about their clients in order to provide the best possible guidance. Clients want to know their advisors are interested in them, understand them, and grasp what they consider important.

Pay special attention to your first conversation with a client; it sets the tone for the relationship. The way you communicate is more important than what you say. The most important skill an advisor must learn is the art of listening. Being patient and allowing for periods of silence is uncomfortable for most people, but it is essential for advisory professionals.

Most financial advisors need to improve their communication skills. This is not always easy; you have had a lifetime developing bad habits. We have practiced the communication techniques advocated in this chapter for years, and we still fall short of our goals. It takes much work to improve your communication abilities, but the benefits last a lifetime. Your clients will be happier, and in the end, so will you.

CHAPTER 7

Looking Forward —
The Future for Advisors

Financial Advisors Must be Willing to
Continually Change Their Strategies

There will be significant shifts in the distribution of wealth in the United States among demographic groups defined by age, ethnicity, gender, education, marital status, location, and profession. Financial advisors need to understand demographic and economic trends in order to target the most promising clients. Married women, Latino and black Americans will continue to improve financially, but wealth will increasingly be concentrated in the hands of older Americans, those with high levels of formal education, and those who work in particular industries, occupations and geographic regions.

231

Growing Population

The United States population grew very rapidly in the latter half of the 20th century, due mostly to a rising birthrate and increasing immigration. Population growth was fairly constant from 1950 to 1990, between 22 and 28 million each decade. The high birthrate accounted for most of the growth from 1950 until 1980. Increasing immigration offset declining birthrates after 1980 and contributed to a 13.1 percent jump in the population in the 1990s, an increase of 32 million people. The U.S. population has grown by almost 50 percent since 1970. Census data projects that the population will grow from about 205 million in 1970 to 295 million in 2005. The population will continue to grow in the future, but at a slower rate. After 2030, the rate of increase in the population could be the lowest since the Great Depression. Nevertheless, using the Census Bureau's medium projections, U.S. population is expected to grow to 400 million by 2050.

There are not only more people, but also more people working in the United States than ever before. The number of people and the percentage of the population in the labor force both increased between 1970 and 2002. The total civilian labor force, ages 18 to 65, grew by 75 percent, from 79 million in 1970, to 145 million in 2002. Sixty-six percent of the population was in the workforce in 2002, compared to 60 percent in 1970. By 2010, it is projected that 67.5 percent of the population will be in the workforce. Much of the increase can be attributed to the growing number of women in the workforce.

Ageing Population

Lower birth rates and longer life expectancy will

result in a steady increase in the average age of the U.S. population. The median age of people in the United States has risen from 30 years of age in 1980 to 35 in 2002, and is projected to reach 38 by 2030. Life expectancy in 1900 was just under 50 years. By the time Social Security was enacted in 1935, life expectancy had climbed 20 percent to about 60 years of age. The percentage of people living to 85 years and beyond will nearly triple by mid-century, from 1.7 percent of the population in 2005 to 21 million people representing 4.8 percent of the population by 2050. The number of people 65 years and older will increase from 35 million in 2005 to 87 million by 2050. The number of retired persons will constitute 12.6 percent of the U.S. population in 2005, and is expected to jump to 20.3 percent in 2050.

In the last 100 years, each generation has been more highly educated and financially successful than the previous generation. Early in the 20th century, many people went no further than the eighth grade, which was all that was required at the time, as the economy mostly consisted of farming and manufacturing operations. As the economy became more service-oriented, greater education was required. Government programs like the G.I. Bill, which enabled many poor Americans to further their education after World War II, as well as increasing government investments in education and government-guaranteed student loans, improved educational opportunities for Americans. This is one trend that may not continue in the future. Although Americans will continue to improve educationally, their economic opportunities and ultimate financial success may not rival previous generations.

Historically, the elderly constituted one of the largest groups of people living in poverty in the United States. In the 20th century, there has been a dramatic shift in wealth that has decreased the number of older Americans living in poverty. From 1950 through the 1990s, wages increased and the economy improved. Working people were better able to put aside some of their earnings for retirement. An abundance of investment opportunities were introduced that enabled them to increase their retirement savings. New retirement plans were created, some of which were invested in the growing financial markets. Social programs like Social Security and Medicare also benefited the elderly. The trend has accelerated in recent years. While the poverty rate for people 18 to 64 was virtually unchanged between 1989 and 1999, the poverty rate for those 65 to 74 years in age decreased from 10.4 percent to 8.5 percent. The largest decline in the poverty rate during this period was for those 75 years or older, which dropped from 16.4 percent to 11.5 percent.

The rising age of the U.S. population and the decreasing percentage of the population in the workforce will have a significant impact on the U.S. economy and the financial strength of older Americans. Retirement income is going to become a much larger part of general U.S. household income. Many more people will survive on income from corporate retirement plans, 401(k) plans and income from retirement savings and Social Security.

As the average age of the population increases, and the number of retired persons rises, the percentage of the population that is in the workforce will continue to decrease. Although more people are able to work past the age 65, most will not, and any small gains in the workforce attributed to older working Americans will be more than offset by the shrinking percentage of the population that will be of traditional working age, from 16 to 64, which is expected to drop from about 58 percent currently to about 50 percent by the middle of the 21st century.

When Social Security was introduced, life expectancy was less that the 65 years of age, the retirement age specified for Social Security and most private retirement benefits. Few people lived to 85 years of age when the program was first established. Social Security payments were manageable because few people reached retirement age. When people did reach 65 and retired, they lived on average only a few more years.

Social Security is considered a retirement account, but it does not adhere to the structure of most retirement plans because it is mostly a "pay as you go" program. Most retirement plans accumulate money as a person works, and then pays that individual out of a fund of accumulated assets. While there is a Social Security trust fund, the majority of social security payments come from current payroll taxes. The trust fund is a cushion that is frequently tapped by the federal government to finance the national debt. Since Social Security was introduced, the U.S. has had a diminishing ratio of workers to retired people. When Social Security was introduced, there were 40 workers for every retired American. The number of workers for each retired person in the United States is expected to fall to about 3.4 by 2008, and 2.5 by 2050. Eventually, there won't be enough income going into the system to support Social Security payments. Recent projections by the Social Security Administration and the Congressional Budget

Office estimate Social Security will run out of money by sometime before the middle of the 21st century.

The marital status of older Americans has shifted in the last 50 years and will continue to change as people live longer. More retired people will be single in the future, not because they're widowed, but because they're divorced. As men live longer, there has been and will continue to be a decrease in the number of retired women who are widowed, and an increase in the number of retired women who are divorced and remain single, as older men tend to remarry more often than women and tend to marry younger partners.

The growing number of single retired people also reflects a generally growing acceptance of divorce in the United States, and a change in the attitude toward retirement. Books like "Age Wave" by Ken Dychtwald and Malcolm Gladwell's "The Tipping Point" describe the change in American attitudes toward retirement. Americans once viewed their lives as just about over when they retired, but as the longevity and health of older Americans has increased, many have come to see retirement as a new chapter in their lives, one in which they might not be with the same partner. People expect to live 20 years after they retire, and are more willing to make significant changes in their lives after retirement.

Greater Diversity
Rising immigration and declining birth rates will continue to increase the cultural and ethnic diversity of the U.S. population, which will accelerate as more primarily white, non-Latino baby boomers die. The white, non-Latino American population will fall in absolute

numbers and as a percentage of the total population. Non-Latino whites currently represent about 70 percent of the nation's population, down from over 85 percent 50 years ago. Census Bureau projections suggest that by 2050, the white, non-Latino population of the country will fall below 50 percent of the total population. California has already dropped to about 50 percent. According to a March 18, 2004 Los Angeles Times story that cites a Brookings Institute report and new Census Bureau data, racial diversity will accelerate in the next half-century. Both Latino and Asian population are expected to triple between 2000 and 2050. By 2050, the rest of the country will look like California does today, and in California, Latino could become the majority ethnic group.

Immigration will help keep the United States population growing in the next 50 years, while Japan and Europe are expected to lose population. The rate of immigration has had two long consistent trends in the last century. Immigration was strong early in the century, over 10 percent in the first decade. A dramatic drop in the 1930s was largely due to the Great Depression. There was no work available for the existing population and immigrants had almost no chance of finding a job. Immigration declined to a level of 0.4 percent by 1940. Immigration has increased each decade since the 1950s, when 2.5 million people immigrated to the United States. In the 1960s, 3.3 million immigrants entered the United States, 4.5 million in the 1970s, 7.3 million in the 1980s, and 7.6 million in the 1990s. Projections show continued growth in the first half of the 21st century. The U.S. population is projected to grow from 295 million in 2005 to 400 million by 2050. Of the 105 million people added to the population, 40 million are expected to come from immigration.

Ricardo Alonso-Zaldivar wrote in the Los Angeles Times that rising immigration will benefit retired Americans as younger tax-paying workers sustain programs that benefit the elderly, such as Medicare and Social Security. Edward Telles, a UCLA sociologist, said, "It's going to be immigrant labor supporting the aging white population."

Prior to 1920, immigrants were predominantly from Europe. Immigration sources shifted to other parts of the world through the 20th century, with significant increases from Latino and Asian countries. Most recent immigration has been from Mexico, and much of that immigrant population has settled in California, Texas, and other border states. Immigrants tend to initially settle in geographic areas where there are already large concentrations of people from their native countries. California, Illinois, New York, New Jersey and Florida now have large immigrant communities with second and third generation ethnic populations.

There is an increase, however, in the spread of ethnic variation throughout the country. Significant Latino populations are increasingly found in many Midwestern, Southern and Northeastern states. The dispersion of immigrants throughout the country is especially noticeable in the Southern United States. William Frey, a demographer at the Brookings Institute, said in a Los Angeles Times article, "The West will have a much stronger Mexican and Latin flavor, but in the South, the black population is moving back. However, it is not growing nearly as fast as the Asian and Latino population. The South will become more multi-ethnic. In the

Northeast, Midwest and Plain states, you will see more of the aging white population."

Not only has the ethnic and racial composition of the United States changed in the last 50 years, but the way Americans classify and consider race and ethnicity has also changed. Twenty years ago, Latinos were not designated as a separate category in census statistics; they were included among whites and Caucasians. The Census Bureau now separates white non-Latinos and white Latinos into distinct categories. Changes in social correctness, reporting trends, and rates of intermarriage will continue to affect the way ethnic and racial data and identity are considered.

Because ethnic identity is complex, mutable, and is self-reported in census data, it is increasingly difficult to interpret ethnic and racial statistics. In the most recent census, it was determined that some white Latino respondents classified themselves as "white," while others considered themselves "Latino." As intermarrying has increased, people frequently do not identify themselves with a single, distinct racial or ethnic group. New categories have been added to census forms to cope with these changes, including "two or more races" and "other race or ethnic group", but many people simply refuse to be classified. Increasing numbers of Americans consider themselves to be a mixture of four or five equally important designations, which has flummoxed data collectors. The great American "melting pot" no longer only refers to the co-existence of people from different ethnic and racial groups; it now also refers to the co-habitation, co-marrying and biological co-mingling of ethnic and racial groups.

There is increasing wealth, education and representation in the workforce of blacks and Latinos. The number of Latinos in managerial and professional jobs has more than doubled in the last 20 years, and is now about the same level as their representation in the overall population. Average black household income in the United States represented 57.6 percent of total average household income in 1980. By 2000, it had increased to 67.6 percent. In constant 2001 inflation-adjusted dollars, black median income increased $7,500 since 1980, while white household income increased $6,500.

However, the measure for mean household incomes shows a different picture. Black incomes rose $10,823, while white mean incomes increased $15,925. Poverty continues to be more prevalent among minorities. The Census Bureau classifies 12.4 percent of Americans as poor; 8 percent of whites; 12.5 percent of Asians; 17.7 percent of Hawaiian and Pacific Islander; 18.2 percent of "two or more races;" 25 percent of African American, and 25.7 percent of American Indians.

The difference between black median and mean income is an indication of the consistent and significant shift in income to the top 20 percent of earners in the United States, and an even more dramatic shift to the top five percent, which is much more heavily represented by white non-Latino workers. The shift has been even more dramatic for white households. In 1980, white median household income was 85 percent of white mean income. By 2001, median white income had dropped to 73 percent of mean income.

Older populations of Americans will have a greater percentage of white, non-Latino people than younger populations. William Frey predicted there will be two diverging populations, an America that is "white, middle-class and graying," and another America comprised of younger, poorer, non-white people. Frey called it a "racial generation gap."

Women's Wealth

Because women have had greater access to education and more control over child-bearing decisions, and because there has been increasing cultural acceptance of women in the workforce and a greater financial need for two-income households, more women are working. The percentage of men who are in the workforce rose from 65.5 percent in 1970 to 71.7 percent in 2002, a 12 percent increase, but the percentage of women in the workforce went from 43.3 percent to 59.6 percent, a jump of 22 percent. Thirty percent of women are now the primary wage earners in two-income households.

Not only will more women be working, they will be working longer. The percentage of people in the workforce 65 years old and over has been fairly constant in the last 20 years, and is expected to remain so. The percentage of people in the workforce 65 years old and over will rise little from 1980 to 2010, from 19 percent in 1980 to 19.5 percent projected for 2010. The percentage of women 65 years old and over who are in the workforce, however, was 8.1 percent in 1980 and is projected to be 11.1 percent in 2010.

Women who have children have joined the workforce in record numbers. The percentage of married women who have children and hold jobs rose from 40 percent in 1970 to 70 percent in 2002, a 75 percent increase. In 2002, 75 percent of single women who had children were in the workforce. The percentage of women who have children, were widowed, divorced or separated, and were in the workforce in 2002 was the highest of any group, male or female, at 82 percent.

The number of women in managerial and professional jobs has increased 25 percent in the past 20 years — women now hold 50 percent of these higher-paying jobs. Women overall have made significant economic gains in the last 30 years. Married women, however, have done better financially than single women. While income levels have increased for all women, household income has risen faster for married women, which is partly attributable to the rise of two-income households. The number of married women in the workforce has more than doubled between 1980 and 2000. By 2002, the percentage of single women in the workforce was just over 67 percent, while the percentage of married women in the workforce was 61 percent, not considerably less.

The number of two-income households increased 50 percent between 1980 and 2002. Rising household income in the last 20 years is in part due to the increase in two-income families. When a married woman joins the workforce, the number of workers per household is often doubled. As the percentage of single parent households has increased in the last 30 years, they have also represented a growing portion of impoverished households. Single parents with children, particularly single women with children, have always been the group with the highest poverty rates in the nation. Although the poverty rate for households headed by single women with children under 17 dropped 12.1 percent during the 1990s, it is still an unacceptably high 51.3 percent.

Targeting Wealth

Despite the mounting total wealth and increasing number of wealthy people in the United States, the nation's assets will increasingly be concentrated in fewer hands, and financial advisors will face considerable competition for high-value clients. In order to attract clients from among the relatively few high net-worth people in the country, Financial advisors need to understand who and where they will be.

In the last 25 years, the rich got richer and the poor got poorer. U.S. median household income has decreased as a percentage of mean household income, suggesting a consistent shift of income to fewer, wealthier households. Between 1980 and 2001, wealthier Americans received an increasing percentage of the nation's total income. In 1980, the lowest 20 percent of American earners received 4.1 percent of the national income. By 2001, they received only 3.5 percent. In 1980, the top 20 percent of American earners received 44 percent of the nation's total income. By 2001, it had risen to over 50 percent.

Wealthier Americans benefited from changes in tax laws over the last 25 years that allowed them to retain increasing portions of their earnings. Average federal income tax rates for the top one percent of earners decreased 7.22 percent between 1980 and 2002, from 34.47 percent to 27.25 percent. By comparison, total average federal income tax rates for all Americans fell only 2.2 percent during the same period, from 15.3 percent to about 13.1 percent. Recent and proposed changes to U.S. tax law will likely shift even more net income to wealthier households, while still allowing all wage earners to keep more of their earned income.

Even with the dramatic increase in two-income households, the American middle class has continued to lose income as a percentage of total national income. In 1987, a single-income household earned about 82 percent of the income of a two-earner household. By 2001, it had fallen to 54 percent. The middle 20 percent of American taxpayers earned 16.6 percent of total national income in 1980 and 14.5 percent in 2001, suggesting middle-class Americans are going to have a more difficult time saving for retirement, and will shoulder an increasing tax burden to support programs like Social Security and Medicare.

On an inflation-adjusted basis, incomes have risen significantly over the past 50 years, while the minimum wage, adjusted for inflation, has actually decreased. The 2000 rate of $5.15 is 35 percent below the 1968 inflation-adjusted peak of $7.92. The current minimum wage has actually declined below the poverty level.

The difference in income between those with varying rates of formal education has dramatically increased. In 1967, people with one to three years of high school earned 95 percent of total national median income and 91 percent of total national mean income. By 1990, their incomes had dropped to 59 percent of the median and 61 percent of the mean.

Household net worth has been steadily rising in the United States. Household net worth is a measure of assets, including houses, investments and pensions, minus liabilities like mortgages and credit card debts. U.S. household net worth peaked at $44.41 trillion in February 2004. The previous peak was $43.58 trillion in the first quarter of 2000, just before the stock market decline.

Increases in household net worth would seem to benefit financial advisors, but the rise is due in many respects to the increase in home values. The median U.S. home value doubled between 1950 and 2000, and rose 18 percent in the last 10 years, from $101,100 in 1990 to $119,600 in 2000. Since the 2000 Census, low interest rates have helped an even greater number and portion of Americans afford a home. As a result, home prices have risen considerably since 2000. However, these assets are not liquid and cannot be invested in securities markets until the house is sold. Even when the home is sold, the remaining assets have often been eroded by debt. Bear Stearns estimated that Americans extracted $491 billion in equity from their homes in 2003, through refinancing and other means.

The number of millionaires in the United States doubled in the last 15 years. Spectrum Group estimates there were about 1.5 million households with a net worth of $1 million or more in 1990, and are about 2.9 million today. Merrill Lynch/Cap Gemini Ernst & Young's 2002 World Wealth report projected high net worth wealth will grow at an average of eight percent per year for the next five years, reaching $38.5 trillion by the end of 2006, not including an estimated $41 trillion in estate assets that will be passed down to future generations in the next 50 years. The report states that less than one percent of the 7.3 million high net worth individuals have "ultra high net worth," which is defined as $30 million or more, suggesting there are 73,000 ultra high net worth individuals. The report claims the number of households with investable assets over $10 million has grown more than 12 percent since 2000, to 100,000 households.

The growing number of wealthy individuals would seem to benefit financial advisors, and it has, which is why so many people have become financial advisors. There are over one million financial services professionals, including 600,000 financial advisors and 400,000 insurance specialists, asset managers, financial planners and others.

The glut of financial advisors has heightened competition in the industry and led to a saturation of the market. There are simply not enough people with enough investable assets to adequately support one million financial advisors. There are almost 14 advisors for every ultra high net worth person nationwide. Even so, ultra high net worth individuals are often not the best clients for financial advisors to target because a large portion of their assets are not actively traded in the securities markets. The Forbes 400 list of the wealthiest people in the country includes many people like Bill Gates and Warren Buffett, whose vast wealth is primarily represented by their companies' stock, which is frequently held for decades or even lifetimes. Many wealthy people's net worth is in real estate that is passed down to spouses, children and other relatives without ever being sold. When transactions do take place, they are likely to involve the buying or selling of large percentages of a company and will be handled by investment banks. Surveys indicate that only 30 percent of investors with $10 million or more use brokers as their primary financial advisors, down from 37 percent in 2001.

There are 7.3 million high net worth individuals in the United States, according to Merrill Lynch/Cap

Gemini Ernst & Young, of which perhaps only half actively trade stocks and mutual funds through financial advisors. There are therefore only three or four high-worth potential clients for each advisor in the country. There are 6.5 million people who own stocks and mutual funds and have $500,000 or more in assets, representing 6.5 clients for each advisor. There are 19 million households in the United States with a net worth of over $250,000, but few of these households have significant investable assets.

There are regional differences in income and operating costs throughout the country. Each financial advisor must determine how many clients at each asset-level they will need to sustain their business. No matter how you parse it, there is a great deal of competition among financial advisors. In order to succeed, financial advisors will need to actively target groups of people who are more likely to be valuable potential clients.

Rising numbers of black, Latino and Asian Americans have become financially successful. New ethnic groups are likely to emerge as ethnic diversity continues to increase in coming years. As members of ethnic groups become more familiar with American culture, and are able to amass investable assets, they are more likely to use traditional financial services. Financial advisors will need to develop the knowledge and skills necessary to serve emerging ethnic, racial and blended cultures.

Despite the economic gains of black, Latino and Asian Americans, however, the country's wealth will still proportionately be in the hands of older white Americans. Age is one of the most important factors in determining who will have wealth in the near future. Most of the nation's wealth is held by people 45 years of age and older. People between 45 and 55 years of age primarily own the homes with the highest estimated value in any given area of the country.

While the nation's wealth is primarily in the hands of older Americans, the country's investable wealth, the kind financial advisors are paid to manage, is concentrated in the hands of very few older Americans. The median net worth outside of pension plans and home equity for people 55 and older is $30,000 or less. Even among more affluent age groups, there is only a small fraction of the population with investable assets that can sustain and justify a financial advisor's time.

Net worth census statistics do not include the value of retirement plans, but increasingly, large corporate pension plans are insufficiently funded to meet their obligations. The underfunding of corporate, state and municipal pension plans is estimated to be in the tens of billions of dollars. Some companies have greater pension fund liabilities than the total net worth of the company. The federal pension benefit guarantee fund does not have sufficient assets to cover the corporate pension plans that are likely to fail. The beneficiaries of many pension plans will receive only a fraction of the retirement benefits they anticipate.

The value of 401(k) and IRA retirement plans declined from 2000 through 2002 along with the equity markets. In many cases, the assets in these plans are at about the same levels as they were five years ago. Many people whose primary retirement funds are held in 401(k) accounts and IRAs will never be able to accumulate the retirement assets they expected.

There is also a rising trend of bankruptcies among older Americans. Historically, people filed for bankruptcy mostly in their 20s and 30s. Today, many people declare bankruptcy in their mid-50s. Many of them have lost well-paying jobs they held for many years in declining industries, and then re-entered the workforce at much lower income levels. Often, they deplete their savings and take on additional debt to maintain their lifestyles. Many have little or no retirement savings and will not have the time or resources to accumulate retirement assets.

In previous generations, women acquired sizable assets only upon the death of their spouses. In the future, women will be earning more of the household income and will have greater investable assets before the death of their partners. Financial advisors will need to improve their ability to attract and serve women clients. Learning as much as possible about educational funds, for example, can be beneficial as women place a high priority on their children's education.

The United States covers 3.5 million square miles and has over 290 million people. This vast country is comprised of distinct regions with very different economic characteristics that can have an enormous impact on financial services professionals. In order to succeed in the future, financial advisors need to be aware of regional economic differences and direct their business activities to areas of the country that are more affluent and highly educated, have greater numbers of wealthy older Americans, and have more vibrant industries and growing populations.

Geographic location has a significant impact on income levels. In 2000, the average per capita income in the United States was $30,413, but there were significant regional variations. The San Francisco Standard Metropolitan Statistical Area (SMSA) had an average per capita income of $45,778, 50 percent higher than the national average, while the Greenville/Spartanburg SMSA had an average per capita income of $25,818.

Population growth has not been equally distributed throughout the United States. There has been a shift of the country's population to coastal and Southwestern states. This is partly due to America's ongoing transition from an agricultural and manufacturing-based economy to a service-based economy. There has been a decrease in the number of farm workers needed to produce agricultural goods and the number of factory workers needed to manufacture goods. Agricultural states and areas of the Midwest that housed manufacturing facilities have seen their populations decline. Service sector jobs are concentrated in major cities, so those states that have the largest percentage of their population residing in cities generally have seen their overall populations grow the fastest. "Quality of life" considerations also play a role. People from cold Northern climates have moved to warmer states to improve their quality of life, especially retirees. Migration from 1995 to 2000 resulted in the Northeast region losing 1,270,858 people, and the Midwest lost 541,189, while the South gained 1,799,799 and the West gained 12,048 people due to migration.

Migration, however, does not account for all of the population changes experienced by regions of the country. While some states, such as California, are experiencing a decrease in migration, increases in immigration from other countries and a high-birth rate are helping the population continue to grow.

Understanding industry and wage trends is critically important for financial advisors, who frequently have many clients in the same industry or profession. Financial advisors will need to focus on those industries that are predicted to grow the most rapidly, and those occupations that are expected to attract the greatest number of workers and command the highest wages. Once an Advisor identifies occupations they want to target, they need to learn which services the people in those occupations most need, and acquire the necessary skills to fulfill their unique requirements.

During the period from 1983 to 2002, U.S. employment grew by 35 percent, adding 35.5 million jobs, about two million jobs per year. However, employment statistics varied widely according to industry and occupation. Economic disparities between states and regions are a function of the industries that reside in those areas. Industries that will continue to decline will affect those regions in which they reside.

The four sectors that have experienced the greatest job losses in the past 22 years, measured as a percentage of the nation's total workforce, are natural resources, manufacturing, transportation and government workers.

There has been a dramatic decrease in the percentage of the workforce engaged in natural resource extraction and manufacturing, and a decline in wages for workers in these industries. The percentage of the U.S. workforce employed in the manufacturing sector has declined from 21 percent to 12 percent in the past 22 years. The number of extraction jobs decreased by half to 100,000. Forestry and logging occupations lost up to 90 percent of their workers. Private household employment, farm operators, machine operators and precision production jobs have also declined. Compensation for manufacturing workers dropped from 130 percent of the median national wage in 1980 to 115 percent in 2002. Regions where concentrations of resource extraction and manufacturing companies are located, primarily in the Midwest, will experience the greatest economic challenges.

The transportation industry has seen its employment numbers decline in absolute terms and as a percentage of the total workforce. The number of government workers has increased, but the percentage of government workers that comprises the total workforce has declined.

Industries that have seen the largest gains in employment, measured as a percentage of the nation's workforce, are the financial, education, health, construction, and leisure sectors. There were only 90,000 managers in the medicine and health fields in 1983, but by 2002, employment in the industry had grown by 790 percent to 800,000. The number of computer scientists grew by 400 percent to two million. The biggest percentage gains in income were in the financial sector. The number of leisure jobs has also been increasing, but the average income level in the industry has held constant at 57 percent of the national median wage.

There are 8.5 million self-employed people in the country. Two-thirds work in the services industries. People who own their own businesses generally do not pay themselves lavish wages and bonuses. They grow their net worth not by saving and investing their salaries, but by building the value of the business.

Home values vary significantly among regions of

country. While the median value for homes in the United States rose 18 percent between 1990 and 2000, the average price in Oregon shot up 77.5 percent, while the average home price in Connecticut declined 26.5 percent. Hawaii continues to have the highest home values of any state. Sunnyvale, California SMSA has an average home price of $495,200, while Flint, Michigan has an average home price of $49,700. Seven of the top 10 SMSAs nationwide with the highest average home prices are in California, while the other three are in Massachusetts, Connecticut and Hawaii. Six cities have over three percent of their homes valued in excess of one million dollars. Cambridge, Massachusetts has 516 homes valued at more than one million dollars, representing 11.6 percent of the housing stock. 547 homes in San Francisco, 7 percent of the housing market, are valued in excess of one million dollars. Pasadena, California has 912 million-dollar homes, 4.7 percent of the market, while Los Angeles has 14,501, 3.8 percent of the market.

In some areas of the country, a significant portion of investable assets may be freed up upon retirement and the sale of a home. A financial advisor's marketing plan needs to take this into consideration. Strategic relationships should be pursued with local realtors who are selling high-value properties.

Competition from discounters and online brokerages, as well as from other financial advisors, will require advisors to attract and service discrete groups of high-worth individuals. In order to effectively service the unique needs of these clients, advisors will require detailed, specialized knowledge, or will need to form partnerships with those who have it. As most wealth will continue in the near future to be in the hands of older Americans, for example, advisors will need to acquire retirement planning and servicing skills.

Because of the increasing concentration of wealthy people who are 65 years old and older, and the tremendous increases in the 75-plus age group, Advisors will need not only more investment and planning skills to deal with their best clients, but will also need to dramatically improve their ability to communicate with older people. Not only will older clients' needs change, but the way they look at the world, the key decisions of control and legacy, will also become more important than the return on their investments. Financial advisors will need more life advisory skills and a greater ability to effectively communicate with their clients. One of their key roles advisors will play will be that of an interface between their clients and their clients' adult children. Dave Solies' book on how to talk to older people should become a primary text for Life Advisors.

Census data suggests that social and demographic changes we are now witnessing will sharply accelerate in the next 30 years. Today's advisors need to emulate Wayne Gretzky, the famous hockey player, who said the secret to his success is that most hockey players skated to where the hockey puck was, while he skated to where it was going. Financial advisors need to be like Wayne Gretzky. They need to track and anticipate social, geographic and demographic changes in order to identify, locate, attract and service the clients necessary to sustain their business.

CONCLUSION

The securities industry has changed dramatically over the past 50 years. Almost every industry in the United States has changed, but few have had the growth and modernization through technology that has been experienced by financial institutions. Investing has changed from the participation of less than 20 percent of the population to an interest by almost everyone in one way or another. Well over half the population has a vested interest in the securities industry.

The only other industry that has experienced as much change is communications. To some extent, the proliferation of the ways people can now communicate and the accessibility of information from the multiple broadcast media largely determines how the securities industry functions. And of course, the Internet has made real-time information available wherever and whenever anyone wants it.

Financial advisors once controlled most of the investment information and therefore had a monopoly on investing information access. Due to the revolution of the communication industry, they have lost that control. Investment retirement plans, proliferation of mutual funds and increased income, along with the growth of the population, have all contributed to a six-fold increase in the number of people investing over the last 50 years.

But this trend has not occurred in a vacuum. The competition in the financial marketplace has increased to the point that no advisor can succeed without achieving a level of excellence in both financial acumen and in managing client relationships that has never before been experienced. And excellence itself has been redefined from doing one thing 1,000 percent better to doing 1,000 things one percent better.

Longevity has increased significantly over the past five decades. Fifty years ago, few people lived to retire at age 65. Those who succeeded had just a few years of retirement to look forward to. There has probably been no single factor impacting our economy more than longevity and the dramatic increase in the percentage of the population who are retired. In 1935, when Social Security was introduced, there were 40 people working for every retired person. The ratio is now 4:1, and census projections anticipate the ratio dropping to 2:1 by the middle of the 21st century. This is going to create some large challenges that Social Security alone is going to have a hard time solving. The need for planning and saving for retirement has become the primary focus for most investors. This is joined in importance by such pressing financial needs as providing for college education and long-term care programs. The new problem people are facing is long years of retirement and concern that they may run out of money before they take the exit door. More people are going to have to rely on retirement income sources other than Social Security

Within all these changes, the role of financial advisors has changed and must change even more. Their services have become much more competitive, diverse and complex. To properly provide service to their clients, they now need a captive or strategic team of specialists to properly service their clients. Clients' needs are much more complex, but the level of personal service has declined, just when serious investors need much higher levels of service. It is now common for financial advisors to provide services to three or more generations of the same family. Successful advisors must master being able to work with a limited number of clients in order to provide the services their best clients rightfully demand.

Because advisors are responding to more and more clients' needs, they are becoming much more involved in their clients' personal lives. We are advocating that the role of an advisor in the future is to become a *Life Advisor*, the central hub directing clients to other professionals who can provide the high-quality service clients want. As a *Life Advisor*, the financial advisor's role will change, the quality of their business will greatly increase, and the personal satisfaction they will receive from practicing their professional will dramatically improve the quality of their own lives.

Never before has any profession been faced with the challenges, the opportunities, or the excitement that this combination of events has created for a financial *Life Advisor.*

INDEX

Index

L

Lefevre, Edwin 88
Levitt, Ted 117
likeability 110, 128, 156, 181, 207

M

Merrill Lynch 31, 49, 67, 91, 97, 245-246
Morgan Stanley 24, 67
Murray, Nick 118, 126, 130
mutual funds 24, 25, 38, 39, 45, 59, 71-77, 79, 86, 247, 256

N

niche marketing 156, 166, 174, 175
Nordstrom 111, 113

O

Optimum Optimorum 139, 151

P

Paine Webber 91
Perry, J. Mitchell 147

R

reciprocity 112, 123, 124, 142, 143, 156, 181, 192-199
Ritz-Carlton 111, 112

S

scarcity 110, 129-130, 156, 181, 188
Securities Act of 1933 24, 94
Separately Managed Account 77-79
Sherman Anti-Trust Act 18, 89
social proof 110, 125-127, 129, 156, 181
social prospecting 158, 186, 189, 191, 193
Social Security 233-236, 238, 244, 256-257
Solie, David 224, 225, 227, 254